CW01594481

# Holiday Wainwrights

## Book One
## The Eastern Fells

RAY PILLING

# INTRODUCTION TO THE SERIES

Long-distance walking trails have become increasingly popular over recent years. 'Bagging' all 214 Wainwrights has also become a popular project for many walkers. The Lake District continues to draw in millions of visitors every year with its beauty and grandeur. This projected series of books will help you to plan and conduct seven fantastic holidays that combine all three of the above interests.

Not everyone is lucky enough to be able to make frequent trips to The Lakes, so, it is important to draw as much from each visit as possible. By walking all of the Wainwrights in a given area in one holiday, you can really squeeze every ounce of enjoyment from your trip to the fells.

The fells refuse to fall neatly into walking days of equal length, but this can be turned into an advantage rather than a nuisance. Make the most of the easy days by spending time relaxing in the beautiful surroundings, but savour the challenge of the longer days.

The fells also refuse to permit a fully logical route through all the peaks. This, combined with walking for several days in a relatively small area of Lakeland, means that you will become very familiar with the peaks and see them from different view-points and distances.

Alfred Wainwright's Pictorial Studies of the Lakeland Fells are an incredible achievement and in walking the Wainwright fells I have visited areas that I would otherwise never have seen.

I hope that these books will serve as a useful companion on your own Wainwright experience and I envy you the journey!

*High Hartsop Dodd from Brothers Water*

# INTRODUCTION TO BOOK ONE – THE EASTERN FELLS

There are 11 itineraries in this book. Each one covers all 35 Wainwrights within The Eastern Fells. The first is named 'Standard 9-Day Itinerary'. The other 10 are named to indicate how they differ:

## 9-Day Itineraries:

Dockray 9-Day Itinerary: The mid-trip overnight stays in Helvellyn Youth Hostel (YH) and Troutbeck are replaced by 2 consecutive nights in The Royal Hotel at Dockray.

Edges 9-Day Itinerary: Dockray is used as above. The main change for "Edges" itineraries is that Swirral Edge is walked on a day that starts and ends in Patterdale, allowing you to carry just a day-pack, and Striding Edge is not walked at all. This might be a better itinerary for those nervous about tackling these two famous ridges.

## No Brothers Water 8-Day Itineraries:

"No Brothers Water" means that Days 1 & 2 of the 9-Day Itineraries are run together to cut out an overnight stay in the Brothers Water Inn.

Standard, No Brothers Water 8-Day Itinerary.

Dockray, No Brothers Water 8-Day Itinerary.

Edges, No Brothers Water 8-Day Itinerary.

## No Ambleside 8-Day Itineraries:

"No Ambleside" means that Days 2 & 3 of the 9-Day Itineraries are run together to cut out an overnight stay in Ambleside.

Standard, No Ambleside 8-Day Itinerary.

Dockray, No Ambleside 8-Day Itinerary.

Edges, No Ambleside 8-Day Itinerary.

## 7-Day Itineraries:

The same overnight stays as the Standard, 8-Day itineraries but without the first overnight stay at Helvellyn YH.

No Brothers Water 7-Day Itinerary.

No Ambleside 7-Day Itinerary.

# HOW TO USE THIS BOOK

## INTRODUCTORY SECTIONS OF THE BOOK

The **SUMMARY STATISTICS** table (pg xi) compares the statistics of the 11 itineraries to help you decide which one to follow.

**THE SUMMITS** are listed in 2 tables (pg xii) – firstly by altitude and then alphabetically.

Refer to the **LUGGAGE**, **TRANSPORT, ACCOMMODATION, MAPS INFORMATION** and **SAFETY CONSIDERATIONS** sections (pg xiv - xix) for advice on planning your trip.

The **OVERNIGHT STAYS** table (pg xx) summarises where you would need to book accommodation for each night of each itinerary.

The **KEYS TO MAPS** section (pg xxii) provides 3 keys to the 3 types of maps used in the book.

The **START/END POINTS OF WALKS** section (pg xxv) contains grid-references for the 7 accommodation places and, for each place, a not-to-scale map giving an indication of where the walk directions begin/end.

All of the measurements given in the book are taken from the OS map. As such, they are accurate enough to describe the walks and give an impression of the difficulty of the day, but are inevitably not 100% accurate on the ground. The measurements were all taken in metric and have been converted to imperial at the following rates:

| 1KM | 0.6 MILES |
|---|---|
| 1M | 3.3 FEET |

Here is a timing chart that you might find useful when estimating.

The timings are in minutes. 0.1 minute = 6 seconds.

| SPEED (KPH) | DISTANCE TRAVELLED (M) | | | | | | | | | | |
|---|---|---|---|---|---|---|---|---|---|---|---|
| | 1000 | 900 | 800 | 700 | 600 | 500 | 400 | 300 | 200 | 100 | 50 |
| 5 | 12 | 10.8 | 9.6 | 8.4 | 7.2 | 6 | 4.8 | 3.6 | 2.4 | 1.2 | 0.6 |
| 4 | 15 | 13.5 | 12 | 10.5 | 9 | 7.5 | 6 | 4.5 | 3 | 1.5 | 0.75 |
| 3 | 20 | 18 | 16 | 14 | 12 | 10 | 8 | 6 | 4 | 2 | 1 |
| 2 | 30 | 27 | 24 | 21 | 18 | 15 | 12 | 9 | 6 | 3 | 1.5 |

## THE ITINERARIES

The Standard 9-Day Itinerary is explained in full. When reading any of the other itineraries, where the route is identical to a previously presented itinerary, the earlier itinerary is referenced.

Each itinerary begins with 3 presentations of information summarising the itinerary:

SUMMARY:

This gives a very brief overview of the structure of the itinerary and which Wainwrights it covers on each day.

ITINERARY MAP:

The Wainwrights are accurately placed in relation to each other and the accommodations. The route for each day is marked to give a visual impression of the itinerary.

DISTANCES, ASCENTS AND MAXIMUM ALTITUDES table:

This shows the daily statistics of the itinerary.

Use these 3 items, in conjunction with your full map(s), to help you decide which itinerary you are going to follow. You might choose to begin the itinerary from another point/day, to reverse it, or even to split it into multiple shorter trips to The Lakes. However, bear in mind that the walk details are written in one direction only.

*Scandale from Little Hart Crag*

# THE DAYS

Each day within the itinerary is covered as follows:

Distance, ascent and maximum altitude for the day.

A summary giving an outline of the route.

A ROUTE MAP to accompany the summary. Please note: **these maps are not intended to be used for navigation and they are not accurate to scale** – they are there to be used in conjunction with your full map(s) when planning the day's walk.

A table showing the map(s) needed, the Wainwrights covered and their heights.

Walk directions split up into sections (usually from accommodation to Wainwright and then fell to fell). Each section begins with its distance and ascent. **The walk directions in this book are not a substitute for a map and compass and the navigational skills to use them**. Timings and route-finding distances are not given. Rather, you are given a series of tick-features to watch out for and instructions on how to proceed from certain points. Where accuracy is required, bearings are given in degrees. Where the route is more obvious or need not be so accurately given, the directions are given in words (eg. north, north-east etc.). Red asterisks are used to mark sections of description referenced by other itineraries.

*Catstye Cam from Hole-in-the-Wall*

# SUMMARY STATISTICS

| ITINERARY | DAYS | DISTANCE | | | | | | | | ASCENT | | | | | | | |
|---|---|---|---|---|---|---|---|---|---|---|---|---|---|---|---|---|---|
| | | TOTAL | | AVE | | MAX | | MIN | | TOTAL | | AVE | | MAX | | MIN | |
| | | KM | MILES | KM | MILES | KM | MILES | KM | MILES | M | FEET | M | FEET | M | FEET | M | FEET |
| STANDARD | 9 | 127 | 79.6 | 14.1 | 8.8 | 20.6 | 12.9 | 9.8 | 6.1 | 8000 | 26400 | 889 | 2933 | 1355 | 4472 | 500 | 1650 |
| DOCKRAY | 9 | 118 | 73.9 | 13.1 | 8.2 | 17.6 | 11 | 9.8 | 6.1 | 7640 | 25212 | 849 | 2801 | 1355 | 4472 | 500 | 1650 |
| EDGES | 9 | 127 | 79.4 | 14.1 | 8.8 | 21.1 | 13.2 | 9.8 | 6.1 | 7490 | 24717 | 832 | 2746 | 1075 | 3548 | 500 | 1650 |
| STANDARD, NO BW | 8 | 126 | 78.6 | 15.7 | 9.8 | 20.6 | 12.9 | 9.9 | 6.2 | 7830 | 25839 | 979 | 3230 | 1355 | 4472 | 500 | 1650 |
| DOCKRAY, NO BW | 8 | 117 | 72.9 | 14.6 | 9.1 | 18.9 | 11.8 | 9.9 | 6.2 | 7470 | 24651 | 934 | 3081 | 1355 | 4472 | 500 | 1650 |
| EDGES, NO BW | 8 | 126 | 78.4 | 15.7 | 9.8 | 21.1 | 13.2 | 9.9 | 6.2 | 7320 | 24156 | 915 | 3020 | 1280 | 4224 | 500 | 1650 |
| STANDARD, NO AMB | 8 | 123 | 77 | 15.4 | 9.6 | 20.6 | 12.9 | 9.8 | 6.1 | 7980 | 26334 | 998 | 3292 | 1355 | 4472 | 745 | 2459 |
| DOCKRAY, NO AMB | 8 | 114 | 71.4 | 14.3 | 8.9 | 17.6 | 11 | 9.8 | 6.1 | 7620 | 25146 | 953 | 3143 | 1355 | 4472 | 745 | 2459 |
| EDGES, NO AMB | 8 | 123 | 76.9 | 15.4 | 9.6 | 21.1 | 13.2 | 9.8 | 6.1 | 7470 | 24651 | 934 | 3081 | 1185 | 3911 | 745 | 2459 |
| NO BW | 7 | 117 | 73 | 16.7 | 10.4 | 25.2 | 15.8 | 9.9 | 6.2 | 7450 | 24585 | 1064 | 3512 | 1530 | 5049 | 500 | 1650 |
| NO AMB | 7 | 114 | 71.4 | 16.3 | 10.2 | 25.2 | 15.8 | 9.8 | 6.1 | 7600 | 25080 | 1086 | 3583 | 1530 | 5049 | 745 | 2459 |

## THE SUMMITS BY HEIGHT

| WAINWRIGHT | M | FEET | GRID REF |
|---|---|---|---|
| HELVELLYN | 950 | 3135 | NY341151 |
| NETHERMOST PIKE | 891 | 2940 | NY343141 |
| CATSTYE CAM | 890 | 2937 | NY348158 |
| RAISE | 883 | 2914 | NY342174 |
| FAIRFIELD | 873 | 2881 | NY358117 |
| WHITE SIDE | 863 | 2848 | NY337166 |
| DOLLYWAGGON PIKE | 858 | 2831 | NY346130 |
| GREAT DODD | 857 | 2828 | NY341205 |
| STYBARROW DODD | 843 | 2782 | NY343189 |
| ST SUNDAY CRAG | 841 | 2775 | NY369134 |
| HART CRAG | 822 | 2713 | NY369112 |
| DOVE CRAG | 792 | 2614 | NY374104 |
| WATSON'S DODD | 789 | 2604 | NY335195 |
| RED SCREES | 776 | 2561 | NY396087 |
| GREAT RIGG | 766 | 2528 | NY356104 |
| HART SIDE | 756 | 2495 | NY359197 |
| SEAT SANDAL | 736 | 2429 | NY343115 |
| CLOUGH HEAD | 726 | 2396 | NY333225 |
| BIRKHOUSE MOOR | 718 | 2369 | NY363159 |
| SHEFFIELD PIKE | 675 | 2228 | NY369181 |
| HIGH PIKE | 656 | 2165 | NY374088 |
| MIDDLE DODD | 654 | 2158 | NY397095 |
| LITTLE HART CRAG | 637 | 2102 | NY387100 |
| BIRKS | 622 | 2053 | NY381144 |
| HERON PIKE | 612 | 2020 | NY355083 |
| HARTSOP-ABOVE-HOW | 580 | 1914 | NY383120 |
| GREAT MELL FELL | 537 | 1772 | NY396253 |
| HIGH HARTSOP DODD | 519 | 1713 | NY393107 |
| LOW PIKE | 508 | 1676 | NY373078 |
| LITTLE MELL FELL | 505 | 1667 | NY423240 |
| STONE ARTHUR | 500 | 1650 | NY347092 |
| GOWBARROW FELL | 481 | 1587 | NY407218 |
| GLENRIDDING DODD | 442 | 1459 | NY380175 |
| NAB SCAR | 440 | 1452 | NY355072 |
| ARNISON CRAG | 433 | 1429 | NY393149 |

## THE SUMMITS BY NAME

| WAINWRIGHT | M | FEET | GRID REF |
|---|---|---|---|
| ARNISON CRAG | 433 | 1429 | NY393149 |
| BIRKHOUSE MOOR | 718 | 2369 | NY363159 |
| BIRKS | 622 | 2053 | NY381144 |
| CATSTYE CAM | 890 | 2937 | NY348158 |
| CLOUGH HEAD | 726 | 2396 | NY333225 |
| DOLLYWAGGON PIKE | 858 | 2831 | NY346130 |
| DOVE CRAG | 792 | 2614 | NY374104 |
| FAIRFIELD | 873 | 2881 | NY358117 |
| GLENRIDDING DODD | 442 | 1459 | NY380175 |
| GOWBARROW FELL | 481 | 1587 | NY407218 |
| GREAT DODD | 857 | 2828 | NY341205 |
| GREAT MELL FELL | 537 | 1772 | NY396253 |
| GREAT RIGG | 766 | 2528 | NY356104 |
| HART CRAG | 822 | 2713 | NY369112 |
| HART SIDE | 756 | 2495 | NY359197 |
| HARTSOP-ABOVE-HOW | 580 | 1914 | NY383120 |
| HELVELLYN | 950 | 3135 | NY341151 |
| HERON PIKE | 612 | 2020 | NY355083 |
| HIGH HARTSOP DODD | 519 | 1713 | NY393107 |
| HIGH PIKE | 656 | 2165 | NY374088 |
| LITTLE HART CRAG | 637 | 2102 | NY387100 |
| LITTLE MELL FELL | 505 | 1667 | NY423240 |
| LOW PIKE | 508 | 1676 | NY373078 |
| MIDDLE DODD | 654 | 2158 | NY397095 |
| NAB SCAR | 440 | 1452 | NY355072 |
| NETHERMOST PIKE | 891 | 2940 | NY343141 |
| RAISE | 883 | 2914 | NY342174 |
| RED SCREES | 776 | 2561 | NY396087 |
| SEAT SANDAL | 736 | 2429 | NY343115 |
| SHEFFIELD PIKE | 675 | 2228 | NY369181 |
| ST SUNDAY CRAG | 841 | 2775 | NY369134 |
| STONE ARTHUR | 500 | 1650 | NY347092 |
| STYBARROW DODD | 843 | 2782 | NY343189 |
| WATSON'S DODD | 789 | 2604 | NY335195 |
| WHITE SIDE | 863 | 2848 | NY337166 |

# LUGGAGE

As there are no baggage-carrying companies for these routes, you have to consider how you will carry all you need for the trip. Obviously, the more you carry, the harder it becomes. The usual advice is to carry no more than $^{1}/_{3}$ of your body-weight, but you should be aiming for much less than that.

There is often a trade-off between weight and expense, and only you can say where you will pay more to save weight. So, here are some tips for ways to lighten the load and potentially increase your enjoyment of the holiday. Above all, remember to pack as light as possible.

- Ask yourself, "Do I really need it?". If the answer is "No", then don't pack it.
- Try only to carry gear needed for that day. If you are in the same accommodation for two or more consecutive nights, you can obviously leave your gear there during the day's walk. But also consider asking if you can leave some gear there if you will be back in two or three days' time.
- Use local taxi companies as baggage-carriers on some or all days.
- Use YH laundry facilities rather than carrying enough clothes to always have some fresh.
- Don't carry snacks enough for the entire trip. Get a packed lunch each day. This will also help the local economies rather than the big supermarket near your home.
- Don't take a towel. B&Bs provide one and hostels can rent you one.

*Grisedale from Grisedale Tarn*

# TRANSPORT

Every year, millions of car journeys are made into the Lake District. On busy days, the roads can be jammed up and there are always cars parked in remote spots whilst people are out doing walks. This is an understandable downside to the popularity of the Lakes and in many ways is unavoidable. However, when planning your holiday, you have the opportunity not to add to the car numbers by using public transport. Another advantage of travelling to and from the Lakes on public transport for your holiday is that you don't need to find somewhere to park the car and don't need to worry that it is safe. So, why not leave the car at home and feel like your holiday has started as soon as you leave the house?

Ambleside is relatively accessible. It can be reached by bus from Windermere or from Penrith via Keswick. Windermere and Penrith are both on the national rail network. If you choose to start and end your itinerary in any of the other overnight locations, then you can use the following sites to plan your journey.

You can find information on Cumbrian buses here:

**www.cumbria.gov.uk**

by following the links to the bus timetables.

You can find train details here:

**www.nationalrail.co.uk**

You can also reach Ambleside by coach and details can be found here:

**www.national-coach-travel.co.uk**

# ACCOMMODATION

The Youth Hostel Association (YHA) has hostels in Ambleside, Grasmere, Patterdale and, crucially, near Glenridding (Helvellyn YH). Note that the Ambleside hostel is about a mile away from the town centre at the end of Lake Windermere – so, you could be adding a mile or two to your walks depending on which itinerary you choose. The YHA website is at **www.yha.org.uk**

The benefit of staying in youth hostels is that they help keep the cost down and are geared to the needs of walkers – in particular, they have drying rooms.

If you don't wish to stay in youth hostels, then here is a bit more information on the various overnight locations including those without a youth hostel. Internet-searching is a convenient way to find accommodation.

## Ambleside

Ambleside is a large town with lots of accommodation of various types and prices. There is also an independent Backpackers hostel.

(**www.amblesidebackpackers.com**)

## Brothers Water

The only option at Brothers Water is the Brothers Water Inn which does B&B.
(**www.sykeside.co.uk/inn.htm**)

## Grasmere

Grasmere is a town with several accommodation options. There is also an independent hostel just out of town. (**www.thorneyhow.co.uk**)

## Patterdale

Patterdale is a small village, but it has a pub that does B&B
(**www.thewhitelioninnpatterdale.co.uk**)

and a hotel (**www.patterdalehotel.co.uk**) as well as a couple of other B&Bs.

There is a Post Office that has a well-stocked shop for packed lunch items.

*Ullswater from Glenridding Dodd*

**Glenridding**

Although not planned in the itineraries, if you decide to stay in Glenridding rather than Helvellyn YH or Patterdale, you can find several options on the internet.

**Dockray**

The only option in Dockray is The Royal Hotel which does B&B. (**www.the-royal-dockray.co.uk**)

**Troutbeck**

Troutbeck is a small hamlet, but you have a choice between a B&B (**www.netherdene.co.uk**)

and a pub (**www.thetroutbeckinn.co.uk**).

# MAPS INFORMATION

## Ordnance Survey (OS) - (www.ordnancesurvey.co.uk)

The Lake District is covered by:

4 *Explorer* maps at a scale of 1:25000. (OL4, OL5, OL6, OL7). These are the maps that I use and they are referenced within this book. They are available from outdoor shops, bookshops and online retailers;

4 *Landranger* maps at a scale of 1:50000. (Sheets 89, 90, 96, 97). The smaller scale of these maps makes navigating much more difficult in my opinion, particularly in mist.

Another option available from OS is to have a map custom made at either 1:25000 or 1:50000 scale. This would allow you to create map(s) centred as you wished with either 20km x 20km or 40km x 40km ground coverage.

## Harvey – (www.harveymaps.co.uk)

Walkers' maps at various scales:

the *Lake District British Mountain Map* covers all the fells at a scale of 1:40000 with 1:20000 enlargements of Scafell and Pillar;

6 *Superwalker* maps cover the whole Lake District at a scale of 1:25000;

2 summit maps at a scale of 1:12500, Scafell and Helvellyn, which some walkers might find useful in poor visibility;

the *Lake District Outdoor Atlas* covers the whole Lake District at the 1:40000 scale.

## SAFETY CONSIDERATIONS

The aim of this holiday is not to complete the itinerary or die trying! The idea is to have an enjoyable but safe holiday. You will be walking in remote terrain where an accident or problem can have serious consequences. It is beyond the scope of this book to give a full lesson in mountain safety, but here are a few points that should be stressed.

The weather in The Lake District is extremely changeable and the likelihood of experiencing only good weather is tiny. So, you must be prepared for the worst, even in summer. That means not only carrying clothing for all weathers, but also being willing to alter the day's plans as late as the morning of the walk. You can get a specialised mountain-weather forecast at **www.mwis.org.uk** if you have access to the internet. (Remember that you might not always get a mobile signal in some parts of the Lake District.) YHs usually have a daily printout of this forecast near reception.

If the weather or forecast is simply too bad or dangerous for venturing onto the fell-tops (eg. lightning storms), please consider how to more safely reach the evening's objective. As almost every day in these itineraries is a linear walking day, you do need to get to the next night's accommodation, but you don't have to take dangerous risks with the weather to get there. Options to consider as enforced alternatives are taxis; public transport; walking earlier or later in the day; and walking a lower level route (such as using passes and valleys between peaks) to avoid the summits. You could return in the future to bag the Wainwrights that you were forced to miss.

If you have problems on the fells and are unable to get yourself to safety, you can call Mountain Rescue on 999 or 112 (ask for the police) – be prepared to give a six-figure grid reference for your location. Details of the Lake District Mountain Rescue Association can be found on the internet at **www.ldsamra.org.uk**

For attracting help from people nearby, the recognised signal is 6 shouts or whistle-blasts repeated at one-minute intervals The response is 3 shouts or whistle-blasts repeated at one-minute intervals. Keep signalling until help arrives. In darkness, the pattern is the same but you can use your torch as well as, or instead of, sound signals.

Remember to carry a first aid kit. If you have some first aid training, so much the better, but even if you don't, the kit could be useful to treat your own injuries or those of somebody else.

# OVERNIGHT STAYS

| DAY | STANDARD 9-DAY | DOCKRAY 9-DAY | EDGES 9-DAY |
|---|---|---|---|
| 0 | AMBLESIDE | AMBLESIDE | AMBLESIDE |
| 1 | BROTHERS WATER INN | BROTHERS WATER INN | BROTHERS WATER INN |
| 2 | AMBLESIDE | AMBLESIDE | AMBLESIDE |
| 3 | GRASMERE | GRASMERE | GRASMERE |
| 4 | PATTERDALE | PATTERDALE | PATTERDALE |
| 5 | HELVELLYN YH | DOCKRAY | DOCKRAY |
| 6 | TROUTBECK | DOCKRAY | DOCKRAY |
| 7 | HELVELLYN YH | HELVELLYN YH | PATTERDALE |
| 8 | PATTERDALE | PATTERDALE | PATTERDALE |
| 9 | AMBLESIDE | AMBLESIDE | AMBLESIDE |

| DAY | STANDARD NO BROTHERS WATER 8-DAY | DOCKRAY NO BROTHERS WATER 8-DAY | EDGES NO BROTHERS WATER 8-DAY |
|---|---|---|---|
| 0 | AMBLESIDE | AMBLESIDE | AMBLESIDE |
| 1 | AMBLESIDE | AMBLESIDE | AMBLESIDE |
| 2 | GRASMERE | GRASMERE | GRASMERE |
| 3 | PATTERDALE | PATTERDALE | PATTERDALE |
| 4 | HELVELLYN YH | DOCKRAY | DOCKRAY |
| 5 | TROUTBECK | DOCKRAY | DOCKRAY |
| 6 | HELVELLYN YH | HELVELLYN YH | PATTERDALE |
| 7 | PATTERDALE | PATTERDALE | PATTERDALE |
| 8 | AMBLESIDE | AMBLESIDE | AMBLESIDE |

| DAY | STANDARD<br>NO AMBLESIDE<br>8-DAY | DOCKRAY<br>NO AMBLESIDE<br>8-DAY | EDGES<br>NO AMBLESIDE<br>8-DAY |
|---|---|---|---|
| 0 | AMBLESIDE | AMBLESIDE | AMBLESIDE |
| 1 | BROTHERS WATER INN | BROTHERS WATER INN | BROTHERS WATER INN |
| 2 | GRASMERE | GRASMERE | GRASMERE |
| 3 | PATTERDALE | PATTERDALE | PATTERDALE |
| 4 | HELVELLYN YH | DOCKRAY | DOCKRAY |
| 5 | TROUTBECK | DOCKRAY | DOCKRAY |
| 6 | HELVELLYN YH | HELVELLYN YH | PATTERDALE |
| 7 | PATTERDALE | PATTERDALE | PATTERDALE |
| 8 | AMBLESIDE | AMBLESIDE | AMBLESIDE |

| DAY | NO BROTHERS WATER<br>7-DAY | NO AMBLESIDE<br>7-DAY |
|---|---|---|
| 0 | AMBLESIDE | AMBLESIDE |
| 1 | AMBLESIDE | BROTHERS WATER INN |
| 2 | GRASMERE | GRASMERE |
| 3 | PATTERDALE | PATTERDALE |
| 4 | TROUTBECK | TROUTBECK |
| 5 | HELVELLYN YH | HELVELLYN YH |
| 6 | PATTERDALE | PATTERDALE |
| 7 | AMBLESIDE | AMBLESIDE |

# KEYS TO MAPS

## Start/End Points of Days' Walks Maps

NORTH

RIVER, STREAM, BECK OR GILL (DIRECTION OF FLOW)

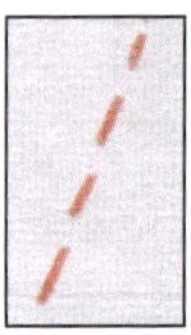
PATH (**NOT** NECESSARILY YOUR ROUTE)

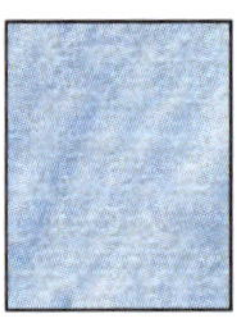
LAKE

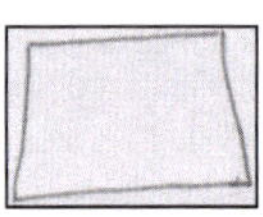
AS INDICATED ON MAP

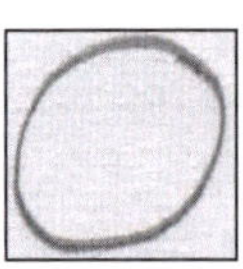
AS INDICATED ON MAP

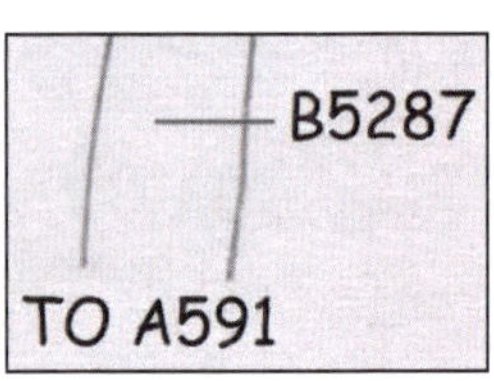

ROAD

## Itinerary Maps

NORTH

WAINWRIGHT

ACCOMMODATION

START OF DAY (NUMBER OF DAY)

END OF DAY

*Ullswater from St Sunday Crag*

## Route Maps

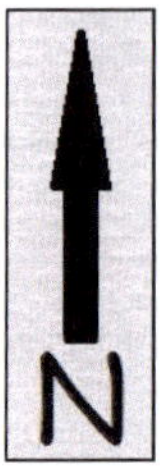

NORTH

WAINWRIGHT (COVERED ON THE ROUTE)

WAINWRIGHT (COVERED ON ANOTHER DAY)

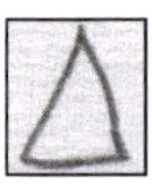
NON-WAINWRIGHT SUMMIT

LAKE OR TARN

RIVER, STREAM, BECK, GILL (DIRECTION OF FLOW)

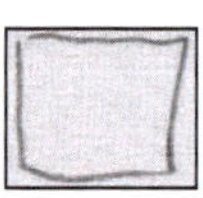
ACCOMMODATION OR BUILDING AS INDICATED ON MAP

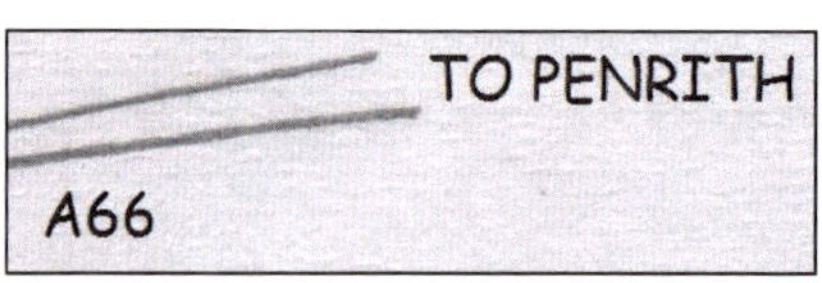

ROAD

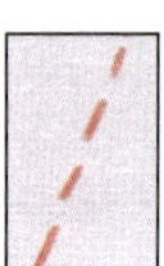
ROUTE

## START/END POINTS OF DAYS' WALKS

These are the locations where the walk descriptions begin and end. When booking your accommodation, consider how to get to and from these points.

| LOCATION | GRID REF |
|---|---|
| AMBLESIDE MINI-ROUNDABOUT NEAR CAR-PARK | NY376047 |
| BROTHERS WATER INN | NY403118 |
| GRASMERE, EASEDALE ROAD | NY337076 |
| PATTERDALE CENTRE | NY398158 |
| HELVELLYN YOUTH HOSTEL | NY365174 |
| DOCKRAY, ROYAL HOTEL | NY392216 |
| TROUTBECK, TROUTBECK INN | NY389271 |

The following maps are not to scale. They are intended only to give an indication as to where to begin/end each day's walk.

## AMBLESIDE

The car-park is to the north of the town centre. The mini-roundabout is at the junction of Rydal Road and Smithy Brow.

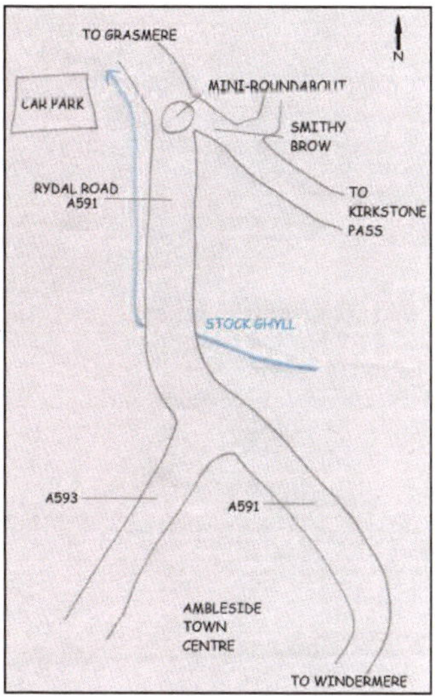

## BROTHERS WATER INN

The Inn is by the A592 just to the south of Brothers Water.

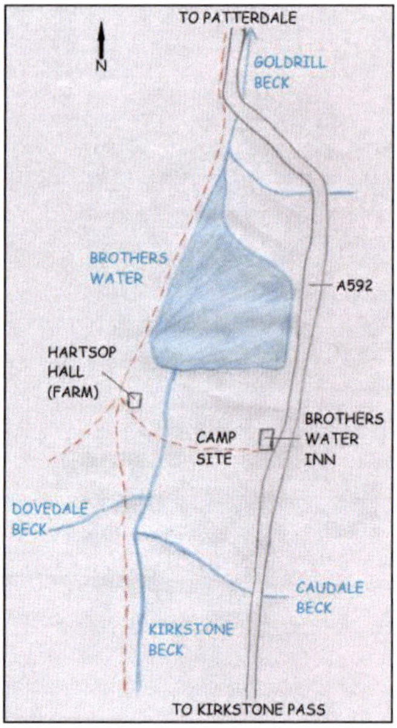


## GRASMERE

Easedale Road begins in the centre of Grasmere.

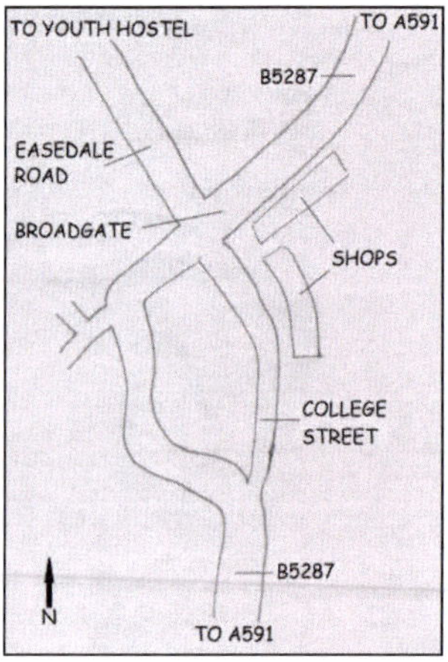

## PATTERDALE

The village of Patterdale is lined up along the A592.

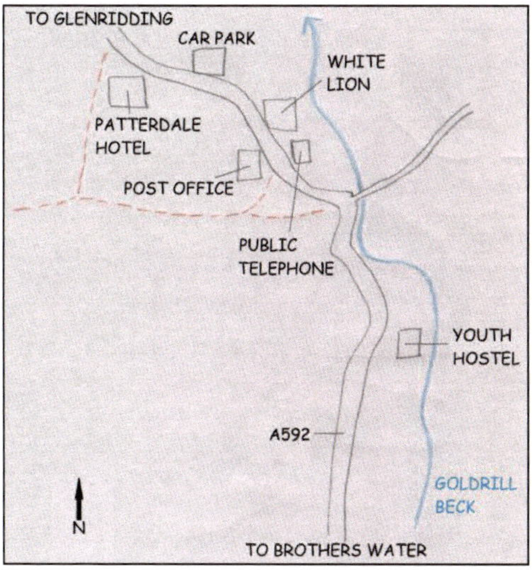


## HELVELLYN YOUTH HOSTEL

The YH is in the Glenridding valley, just over a mile west of Glenridding village.

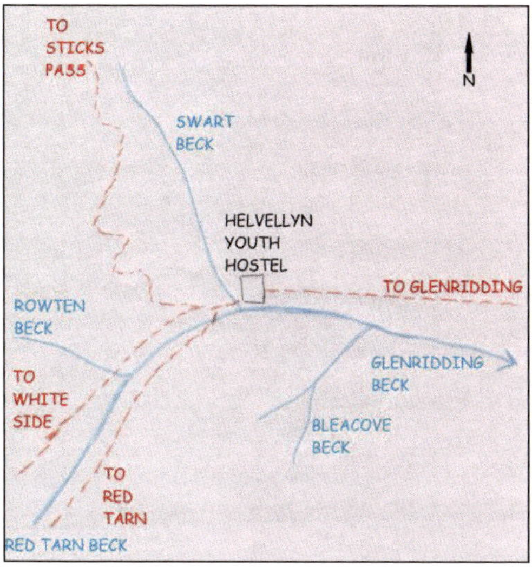

## DOCKRAY, ROYAL HOTEL

The hotel is in the centre of the hamlet of Dockray on the A5091, immediately to the north of the bridge, at the road junction.

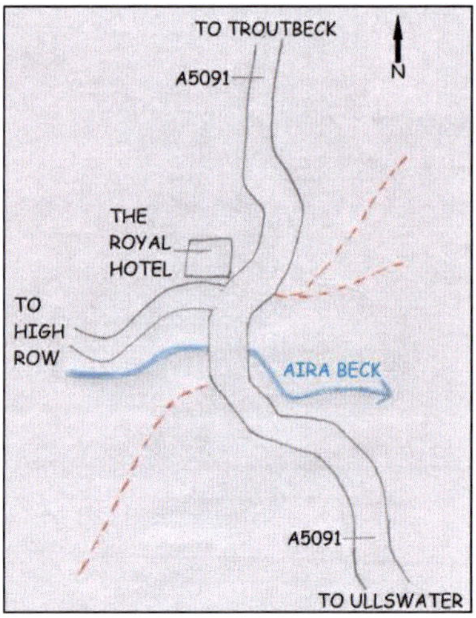


## TROUTBECK, TROUTBECK INN

The Inn is on the A5091 just before the junction with the A66.

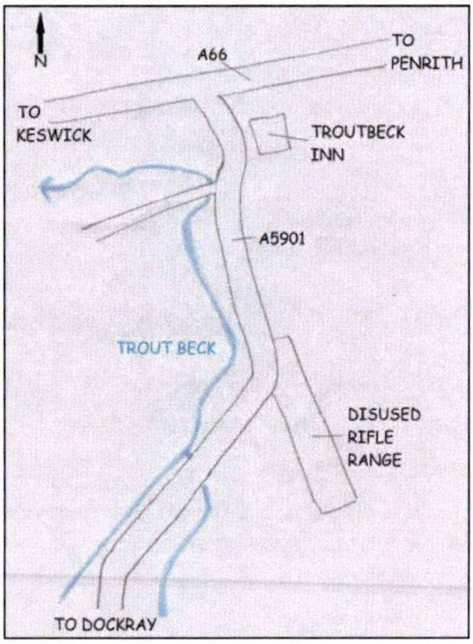

# THE ITINERARIES

# STANDARD 9-DAY ITINERARY

## SUMMARY

**Days 1 & 2** form a loop, heading out over RED SCREES and MIDDLE DODD to an overnight stay at Brothers Water before returning over HIGH HARTSOP DODD, LITTLE HART CRAG, DOVE CRAG, HIGH PIKE and LOW PIKE to Ambleside. 7 Wainwrights done.

**Day 3** moves you on to Grasmere for the night via STONE ARTHUR. 8 Wainwrights done.

**Day 4** takes you over SEAT SANDAL, DOLLYWAGGON PIKE, ST SUNDAY CRAG, BIRKS and ARNISON CRAG to Patterdale. 13 Wainwrights done.

**Day 5** sees you tick off GLENRIDDING DODD, SHEFFIELD PIKE, HART SIDE, RAISE and WHITE SIDE and ends with an overnight stay at Helvellyn YH. 18 Wainwrights done.

**Days 6 & 7** form a large loop, heading out over GOWBARROW FELL, LITTLE MELL FELL and GREAT MELL FELL to an overnight stay at the tiny hamlet of Troutbeck before returning over CLOUGH HEAD, GREAT DODD, WATSON'S DODD and STYBARROW DODD to Helvellyn YH. 25 Wainwrights done.

**Day 8** takes you over CATSTYE CAM, HELVELLYN, NETHERMOST PIKE and BIRKHOUSE MOOR to Patterdale for another overnight stay there. 29 Wainwrights done.

**Day 9** completes the itinerary with a return to Ambleside over HARTSOP-ABOVE-HOW, HART CRAG, FAIRFIELD, GREAT RIGG, HERON PIKE and NAB SCAR. 35 Wainwrights done!!!

*Little Hart Crag from High Hartsop Dodd*

## ITINERARY MAP: STANDARD 9-DAY ITINERARY

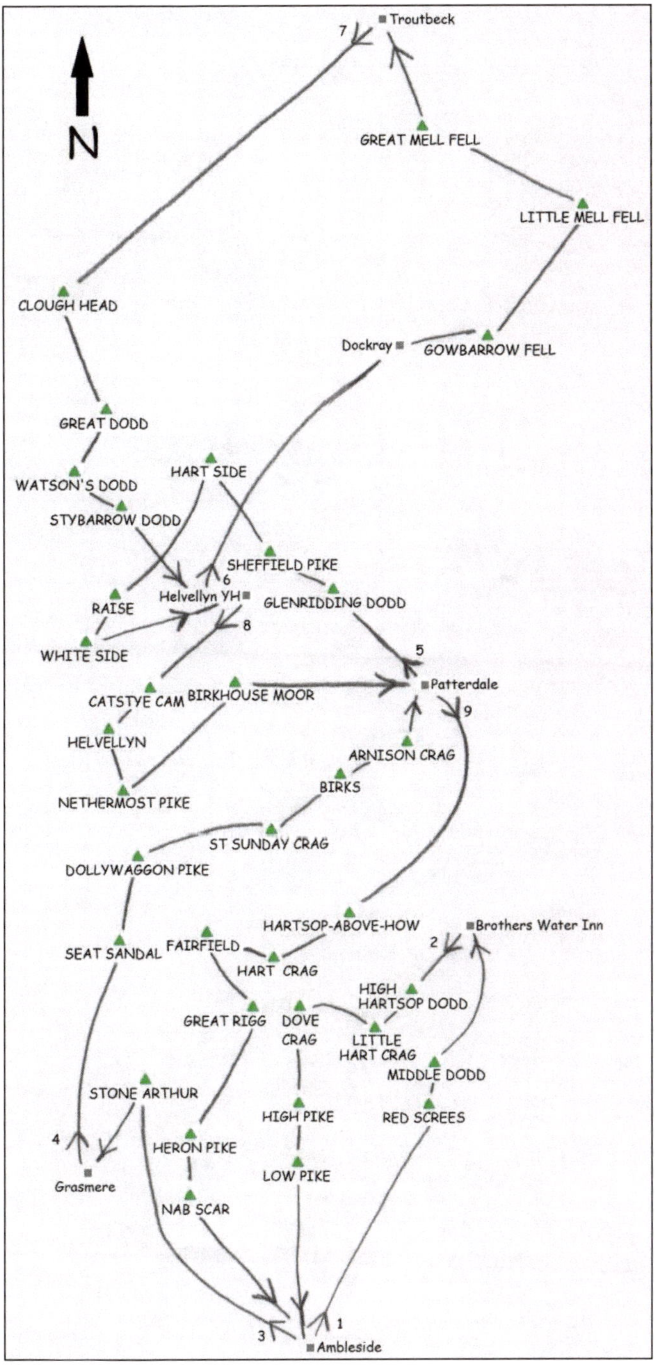

## DISTANCES, ASCENTS AND MAXIMUM ALTITUDES:

### STANDARD 9-DAY ITINERARY

| DAY | FROM | TO | DISTANCE | | ASCENT | | MAX ALTITUDE | |
|---|---|---|---|---|---|---|---|---|
| | | | KM | MILES | M | FEET | M | FEET |
| 1 | AMBLESIDE | BROTHERS WATER INN | 9.8 | 6.1 | 745 | 2459 | 776 | 2561 |
| 2 | BROTHERS WATER INN | AMBLESIDE | 10.7 | 6.7 | 705 | 2327 | 792 | 2614 |
| 3 | AMBLESIDE | GRASMERE | 9.9 | 6.2 | 500 | 1650 | 500 | 1650 |
| 4 | GRASMERE | PATTERDALE | 14.3 | 8.9 | 1355 | 4472 | 858 | 2831 |
| 5 | PATTERDALE | HELVELLYN YH | 14.7 | 9.2 | 980 | 3234 | 883 | 2914 |
| 6 | HELVELLYN YH | TROUTBECK | 20.3 | 12.7 | 1130 | 3729 | 630 | 2079 |
| 7 | TROUTBECK | HELVELLYN YH | 20.6 | 12.9 | 870 | 2871 | 857 | 2828 |
| 8 | HELVELLYN YH | PATTERDALE | 11.5 | 7.2 | 870 | 2871 | 950 | 3135 |
| 9 | PATTERDALE | AMBLESIDE | 15.5 | 9.7 | 845 | 2789 | 873 | 2881 |
| | | **TOTALS** | **127.3** | **79.6** | **8000** | **26400** | | |

# Day 1

## Ambleside to Brothers Water Inn

**9.8km (6.1 miles) distance - 745m (2459 feet) ascent - 776m (2561 feet) max altitude**

**Summary:** From Ambleside, pick up the public footpath that joins Kirkstone Rd at the 150m contour. Leave the road at the 230m contour and climb the ridge over Snarker Pike to RED SCREES. Then descend to MIDDLE DODD and steeply down the ridge to the concessionary path just before Kirkstone Beck. Take the public footpath that runs to the west of the beck to Hartsop Hall (just a farm) and then cross the beck for an overnight stay at the Brothers Water Inn beside the A592 at Kirkstonefoot beyond Sykeside campsite.

**ROUTE MAP: AMBLESIDE TO BROTHERS WATER INN**

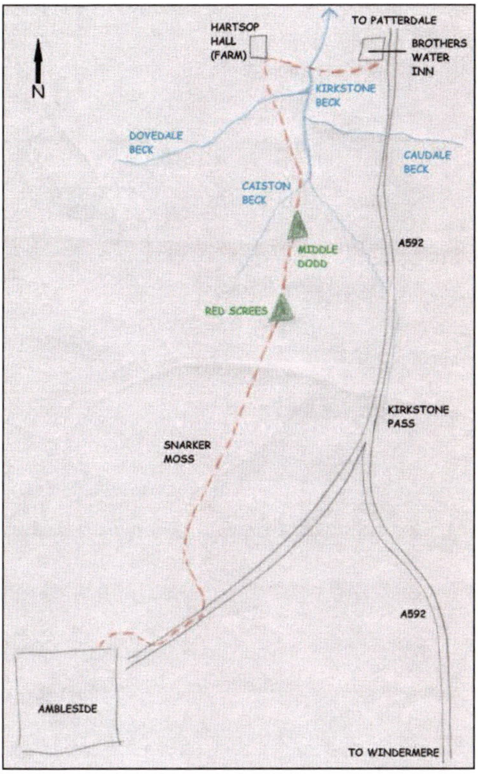


| MAPS | WAINWRIGHTS | M | FEET |
|---|---|---|---|
| OL5, OL7 | RED SCREES | 776 | 2561 |
| | MIDDLE DODD | 654 | 2158 |

## Ambleside to RED SCREES

**5.7km (3.6 miles) distance – 725m (2393 feet) ascent**

**Route:** From the mini-roundabout, go up the road signed "KIRKSTONE 3". Pass the 'Golden Rule' pub and bear left up Kirkstone Road. Turn left onto Sweden Bridge Lane. Continue on, ignoring Belle Vue Lane on the left. At the fork, bear right on Ellerigg Road for the footpath to Kirkstone Road. When you reach the sign pointing left for the public footpath, bear right to join the public footpath for Kirkstone Road.

Go through the gate over the wall and turn right. Go through the gate over the wall and straight on. Go through the gate or over the stile. Follow the track to the road and turn left uphill. Pass between 2 black iron Thirlmere pipeline marker gates. Pass a footpath to the right and a bench.

As the road levels a little bit, take the footpath on the left through a gate. Go through 2 gates and continue up between 2 walls. When the walls turn left, stay on the path (which follows the right-hand wall). Go over a stile and continue up between 2 walls. Go through a gate and continue up between 2 walls. The left wall becomes intermittent, but the right wall is constant. Go over a stile and continue ahead following the wall. When the ground levels out, stay between the walls as they bear left. Continue up by the left-hand wall and go over a stile. Continue straight up ahead.

As the left-hand wall kinks left, your path bears right. As the right-hand wall comes back into view, bear left and follow the wall up. As the wall kicks away to the right, continue on the path straight up. Go over the low wall and continue straight up. Pass 3 cairns. Pass 3 small tarns. RED SCREES summit has a trig point and a wind-shelter.

## RED SCREES to MIDDLE DODD

**1km (0.6 miles) distance - 10m (33 feet) ascent**

**Route:** If the weather is good and you feel confident with the large backpack, you can follow the edge of the sharp drop ahead down to Middle Dodd (roughly 320° initially), but a safer route in strong winds is to take the path leading 300° from the trig point round to the left of the mound with a cairn on, then, soon, at a fork, bear right (350°), then descend at about 300° through sparse boulder patches to a collapsed wall running south-west to north-east.

Turn right and follow the wall north-east. As you reach the corner of the wall, where it turns right and drops steeply to Kirkstone Pass, you meet the path that you could have taken down the edge from RED SCREES. Cross over the wall and follow the ridge to the cairn on MIDDLE DODD.

## MIDDLE DODD to Brothers Water Inn

**3.1km (1.9 miles) distance - 10m (33 feet) ascent**

**Route:** Follow the path straight down the ridge. Cross the broken wall and keep to the path. As the path becomes faint and you see about 5 trees ahead, you **must** bear left to avoid dangerous crags – head over towards the wall running down the hill. As you get round the crags, the path becomes clearer again – follow it to the wall and then follow the wall down to the bottom corner of the field.

A path cuts across and through the wall, turn left to follow it to the footbridge in the corner. Cross the bridge and either continue straight up to meet the path and turn right or cut the corner to meet the path further to the right. You will reach an old barn. This is the point you need to return to tomorrow to commence the ascent of HIGH HARTSOP DODD.

Go through the gate to the right of the barn and follow the path across the field, over the bridge and to the barns at the edge of the field. Turn right and go through the gate on the left after about 20m. Cross the small footbridge, turn right, bear right at the farmhouse and follow the surfaced track to the Brothers Water Inn through the campsite.

# Day 2

## Brothers Water Inn to Ambleside

**10.7km (6.7 miles) distance - 705m (2327 feet) ascent - 792m (2614 feet) max altitude**

**Summary:** From the Brothers Water Inn, head back past Hartsop Hall and take the public footpath south to the foot of the ridge up to HIGH HARTSOP DODD. Climb it and continue up to LITTLE HART CRAG. Use the public footpath to cross Bakestones Moss and then climb to DOVE CRAG (with an optional detour to the viewpoint at High Bakestones). Then, heading south, descend the ridge over HIGH PIKE and LOW PIKE, past High Brock Crags and Low Brock Crags, past High Sweden Bridge and over Low Sweden Bridge, past Nook End Farm and back to Ambleside for an overnight stay.

| MAPS | WAINWRIGHTS | M | FEET |
|---|---|---|---|
| OL5, OL7 | HIGH HARTSOP DODD | 519 | 1713 |
| | LITTLE HART CRAG | 637 | 2102 |
| | DOVE CRAG | 792 | 2614 |
| | HIGH PIKE | 656 | 2165 |
| | LOW PIKE | 508 | 1676 |

## ROUTE MAP: BROTHERS WATER INN TO AMBLESIDE

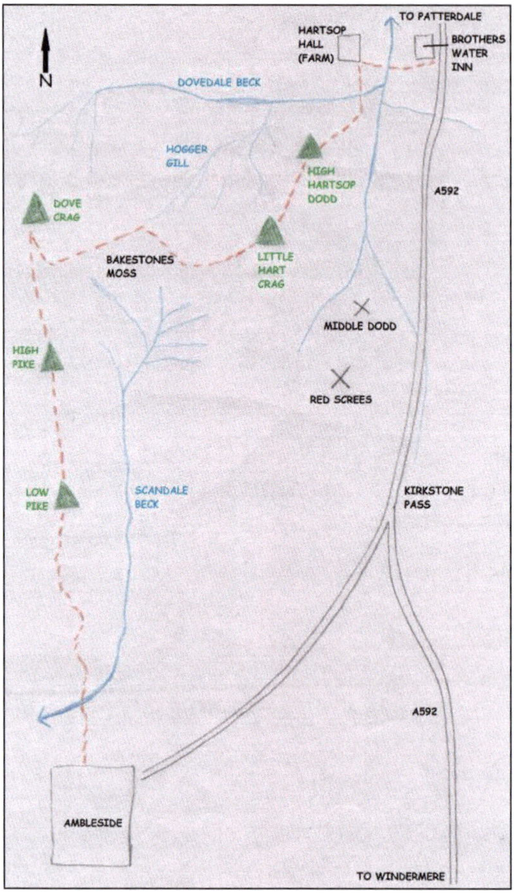


## Brothers Water Inn to HIGH HARTSOP DODD

**2km (1.3 miles) distance - 360m (1188 feet) ascent**

**Route:** From the Inn make your way back to the old barn encountered yesterday at the foot of HIGH HARTSOP DODD.

Take the faint path straight up the ridge. Go over the stile in the fence. Continue up the ridge until you reach a broken wall on your left, follow it just a short way and then cross through the wall and continue up the ridge. There is a small grassy rise and HIGH HARTSOP DODD is marked by a small cairn.

## HIGH HARTSOP DODD to LITTLE HART CRAG

**1km (0.6 miles) distance - 120m (400 feet) ascent**

**Route:** Continue up the ridge and either go over or bypass the first summit and there is a cairn on the second and true summit of LITTLE HART CRAG.

## LITTLE HART CRAG to DOVE CRAG

**1.7km (1.1 mile) distance - 190m (627 feet) ascent**

**Route:** Leave the summit and drop to the path leading roughly west to the fence-posts, turn right and follow the path across Bakestones Moss. Still following the path and the fence-posts, you climb steeply uphill.

[Just before the ground levels out, you have the option of visiting Bakestones cairn which is an excellent viewpoint and a good spot for a break. Turn left off the path and descend (no path) roughly south for about 250m to the large cairn. Afterwards, return to the path by the same route with about 40m height to regain.]

As the ground levels out, you can either turn right to ascend DOVE CRAG more directly or follow the fence-posts to the wall and turn right to follow the wall past a cairn to the cairn on the summit of DOVE CRAG.

## DOVE CRAG to HIGH PIKE

**1.6km (1 mile) distance - 5m (17 feet) ascent**

**Route:** Follow the wall back down. Pass the cairn (again). Cross the fence-posts you followed up. Pass 2 cairns. Pass a wall coming off to the right of the wall you're following.

The ground levels out and you can avoid the boggy ground by crossing through the wall. Follow the wall. There is a slight rise and back on the other side of the wall is a cairn to mark the summit of HIGH PIKE.

## HIGH PIKE to LOW PIKE

**0.9km (0.6 miles) distance - 20m (66 feet) ascent**

**Route:** Stay on the left of the wall and follow it down. Cross the ladder-stile over the wall. The ground becomes level/undulating.

There is a short, steep climb and the wall is at the highest point of LOW PIKE with a small cairn just at the side.

## LOW PIKE to Ambleside

**3.5km (2.2 miles) distance - 10m (33 feet) ascent**

**Route:** Follow the wall down – stay on the path as it doesn't always stick close to the wall. Cross a broken wall. Reach a signpost saying "Deep Bog Path" and pointing right – obey the sign, keep right and follow the wall. Cross a low wall and continue straight on.

The path swings well away to leave the wall, follow the path and leave the wall. Cross a broken wall. Ignore a path descending to the left. Pass a silted up tarn on the right and a sheepfold on the left and go through the wall ahead. Cross a broken wall. Go through 2 walls. Pass a black iron Thirlmere pipeline marker gate on the right and 2 inspection hatches on the left.

Turn right to go through at the end of the wall. The path bends back on itself sharp left round an ash tree* - stay on the path, cross the bridge, go through 2 gates and follow the tarmac road straight on. At the fork keep right, downhill. At the end of the road turn right and you reach the mini-roundabout from where you started yesterday.

# Day 3

## Ambleside to Grasmere

**9.9km (6.2 miles) distance - 500m (1650 feet) ascent - 500m (1650 feet) max altitude**

**Summary:** From Ambleside, a short road-walk north-west on the A591 to Scandale Bridge, followed by a walk through Rydal Park and past Rydal Hall, bring you to the low-level Coffin Route which you take below NAB SCAR (not ticked off until Day 9), past Town End to the outskirts of Grasmere near Michael's Fold. From there, a steep climb on the public footpath takes you up to the day's only Wainwright, STONE ARTHUR. Descending the same way takes you back to Grasmere to finish a short day's walking.

| MAPS | WAINWRIGHTS | M | FEET |
|---|---|---|---|
| OL7 | STONE ARTHUR | 500 | 1650 |

## ROUTE MAP: AMBLESIDE TO GRASMERE

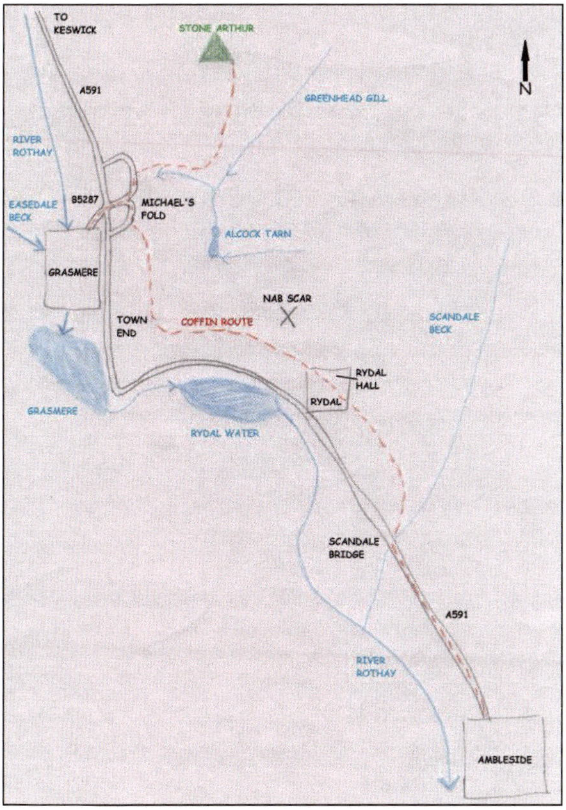


# Ambleside to STONE ARTHUR

**7.6km (4.8 miles) distance - 500m (1650 feet) ascent**

**Route:** From the mini-roundabout, walk away from Ambleside towards Grasmere on the A591. Stay on the left of the road to keep a pavement. Pass the Health Centre. Pass the sign for "KESWICK 16". Go over the river, then cross the road and take the footpath to Rydal Hall to the right of the gate-house.

Continue along this path.* At the sign-posts before the buildings, turn right to follow the 'Coffin Route'. Then turn left to follow the sign for Grasmere. Go through the complex of buildings and past the tea-shop. When you reach the road, turn right and up a very steep short section. Turn left on the public footpath for 'Coffin Route' to Grasmere.

Go through 3 gates. Go past a stone bench and a wooden bench. Go through 2 more gates. Pass another wooden bench. Go through another gate. Continue straight on ignoring a path dropping downhill to the left.

Continue straight on past White Moss Tarn (and watch out for the heron that is often seen there). Turn right onto the public footpath marked "Alcock Tarn 1¼ miles". Join the larger track. Go through the gate into Brackenfell straight ahead.

Go through a gate. Go past a bench. At the T-junction, turn left onto the permitted route. Go through a gate. Cross a little footbridge. Pass a black iron Thilrmere pipeline marker gate on the left and go over a stile. After you pass the corner of the wall, you'll see another marker gate behind you to the left.

Turn left downhill at an arrow sign. Pass a bench on your right. Continue on the path. Go through a gate and pass a bench. Go through a gate and swing round to the left of the house following it round to your right to the gate onto the road.

Turn right. Go over the bridge and then turn right up the road. Turn right onto the public footpath (tarmac) for Greenhead Gill and Alcock Tarn. Continue up by the stream to the end of the road. Go through the gate and turn left for STONE ARTHUR. The path goes up by the wall.

Pass a black iron Thirlmere pipeline marker gate. Turn right uphill at the yellow arrow at the broken wall. The path follows the broken wall, then is between 2 broken walls. Cross the stream and kick right. Pass the solitary sycamore. Eventually the path swings left and the ground becomes more grassy.

When you reach the corner of the wall, bear right uphill away from the wall. Pass a fenced-off mine-shaft on your right. The summit is the top of the crags that are now straight ahead.

Ascend just to the right of the main crag, by following a path off to the left of the path that bypasses the summit. When the ground starts to level out, kick back left up a short grassy rise to the summit which is marked by a tiny cairn to the left of a large boulder.

## STONE ARTHUR to Grasmere

**2.3km (1.4 miles) distance - 0m (0 feet) ascent**

**Route:** Descend the same way you ascended. Follow the road down to the main road (A591). You emerge beside the Swan Hotel. Cross the main road and head down Swan Lane into Grasmere centre.

# Day 4

## Grasmere to Patterdale

**14.3km (8.9 miles) distance - 355m (4472 feet) ascent - 858m (2831 feet) max altitude**

**Summary:** From Grasmere, a short road-walk up Easedale Rd and north past Thorny How hostel takes you to Mill Bridge on the A591, from where, you initially use the public bridleway until about the 170m contour and then climb the shoulder of SEAT SANDAL. From there, you drop steeply and climb steeply (north) up to DOLLYWAGGON PIKE. Then, a steep, zig-zag path takes you down to the eastern end of Grisedale Tarn and you make yet another steep ascent, this time up the flank and ridge of ST SUNDAY CRAG via Deepdale Hause. A steep descent and a gently undulating ascent take you to BIRKS. A steep descent leads you east to Trough Head, then, a final ascent for the day brings you to ARNISON CRAG. You descend by the wall north past Oxford Crag and follow the public footpath east into Patterdale for the night.

### ROUTE MAP: GRASMERE TO PATTERDALE

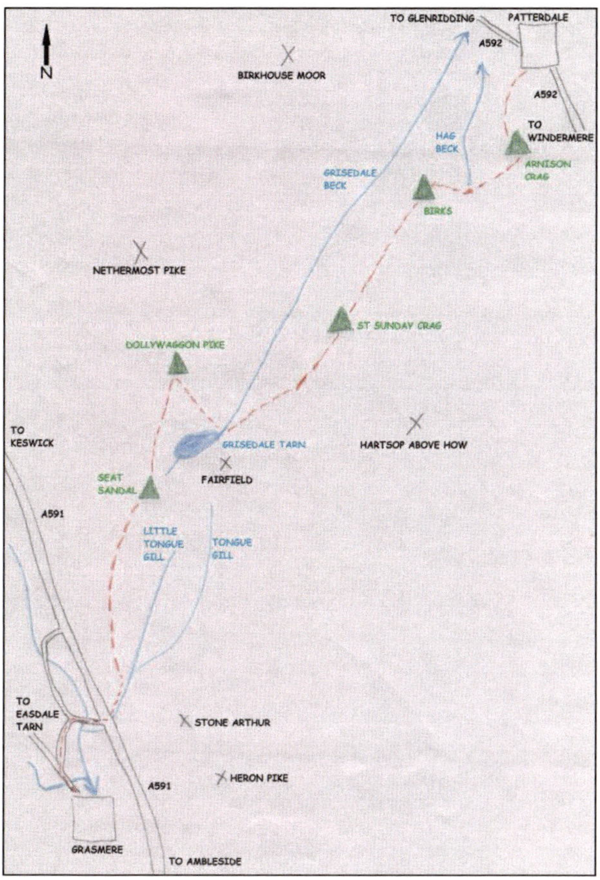

| MAPS | WAINWRIGHTS | M | FEET |
|---|---|---|---|
| OL5, OL7 | SEAT SANDAL | 736 | 2429 |
| | DOLLYWAGGON PIKE | 858 | 2831 |
| | ST SUNDAY CRAG | 841 | 2775 |
| | BIRKS | 622 | 2053 |
| | ARNISON CRAG | 433 | 1429 |

## Grasmere to SEAT SANDAL

**4.5km (2.8 miles) distance - 710m (2343 feet) ascent**

**Route:** Go up Easedale Road [signposted "Easedale Tarn"]. Pass Butharlyp How YH. Turn right [signposted "Thorney How 440yds"]. Pass Thorney How. At the river, turn right and cross the bridge. Continue up to the main road (A591).

Cross the road and go up the public bridleway [signposted "Patterdale"]. Go through a gate. Go through the gate on the left at a barn in the field and turn right uphill. Pick up the grassy farm-track and follow it to the top right-hand corner of the field, go through gate. Continue up the ridge. Go through the gate at the top of the field and continue up the ridge. Go through the final gate onto the open fell and follow up the ridge which arcs left to right to the top.

As you approach the top there are a few cairns. The summit cairn is just before the collapsed wall.

## SEAT SANDAL to DOLLYWAGGON PIKE

**1.6km (1 mile) distance - 290m (957 feet) ascent**

**Route:** Follow the wall down steeply north to the col. (The wall has a long missing section partway down and finishes before the bottom of the col.)* Cross the col and follow the collapsed wall straight up north. The wall ends partway up, but then shortly afterwards there are iron posts to follow.

When the posts stop, you can follow the track straight up and you reach a more ornate iron post and a path cutting across you. Cross over the path and continue uphill. When you reach the cairn, the summit cairn is on a small promontory to the north-east.

## DOLLYWAGGON PIKE to ST SUNDAY CRAG

**3.8km (2.4 miles) distance - 300m (990 feet) ascent**

**Route:** Head back down to the ornate post and turn left on the path which zig-zags down to the outlet stream at the north-eastern end of Grisedale Tarn.** Cross the outlet stream and pick up the path that climbs diagonally to the left up the flank to the ridge of ST SUNDAY CRAG.

When DOLLYWAGGON PIKE is at about 290° from you, watch for and take the path which goes directly uphill to the right, marked by a small cairn. When you reach the ridge at Deepdale Hause, turn left and follow it to the summit cairn.

## ST SUNDAY CRAG to BIRKS

**1.5km (0.9 miles) distance - 20m (66 feet) ascent**

**Route:** Head north-east and pick up the faint path descending the ridge gently. Pass several cairns and it descends a bit more steeply on the ridge on a clear path. It then becomes mostly steep down to a col where the path forks, take the right-hand fork up the grassy rise and over undulating ground to BIRKS, marked by a small cairn.

## BIRKS to ARNISON CRAG

**1.6km (1 mile) distance - 35m (116 feet) ascent**

**Route:** Follow the path that is just north of East for a couple of hundred metres (very approximately) and you reach a small, flat cairn on your left, turn right on a very faint path. When you find the collapsed wall, follow it down to the bottom, cross the stream and turn left on a grassy path.

At the wall, turn right and follow it uphill. When the wall begins to go downhill to the left, follow it briefly but then bear right to keep to higher ground and cross the undulating ground to a col. From here it's a short final climb to ARNISON CRAG, marked by a cairn.

## ARNISON CRAG to Patterdale

**1.3km (0.8 miles) distance - 0m (0 feet) ascent**

**Route:** Return to the col, but turn right just before you reach it and take the path heading down towards Ullswater. The path soon joins the wall and follows it down.

At the bottom of the wall, ignore the gates on the left and stay on the path as it swings right. Go through a gate and the bear right at the fork in the path. Turn right onto the track and follow it down to the toilets and the road (A592).

Turn right for YH, or left for White Lion Inn, Post Office and Patterdale Hotel.

# Day 5

## Patterdale to Helvellyn YH

**14.7km (9.2 miles) distance - 980m (3234 feet) ascent - 883m (2914 feet) max altitude**

**Summary:** From Patterdale, a short stretch of road-walking north on the A592 takes you to Glenridding and just after Glenridding Bridge you turn left up the road past the Travellers Rest pub to the foot of Blaes Crag. You ascend The Rake north to the wall and then a short return journey to the east ticks off GLENRIDDING DODD. From The Rake, you now head north-west over Heron pike to SHEFFIELD PIKE. You now drop to Nick Head and then climb to the east of the disused quarries to head north above Glencoyne Head. This leads you across the col to the summit of HART SIDE. Next, you return to the col and then head south-west to skirt White Stones on its northern side and make your way to the top of Sticks Pass. Make the steady climb south to RAISE. From there, descend and climb south-west to WHITE SIDE (marked as Whiteside Bank) before turning back briefly and turning down to zig-zag down into Glenridding valley and follow down to Helvellyn YH.

| MAPS | WAINWRIGHTS | M | FEET |
|---|---|---|---|
| OL5 | GLENRIDDING DODD | 442 | 1459 |
| | SHEFFIELD PIKE | 675 | 2228 |
| | HART SIDE | 756 | 2495 |
| | RAISE | 883 | 2914 |
| | WHITE SIDE | 863 | 2848 |

## Patterdale to GLENRIDDING DODD

**3.4km (2.1 miles) distance - 290m (957 feet) ascent**

**Route:** Walk the A592 north to Glenridding. After the river, turn left up the road for the Travellers Rest pub and the YH. Pass the Travellers Rest. Stay on the tarmac road when it bends right at Gillside Farm and then also when it bends left as a public footpath leaves it on the right.

Pass the terraced houses and turn right after the cattle-grid up a zig-zag grassy path to the marker post. The path goes up past the telegraph pole and on up to the wall at the col between GLENRIDDING DODD (to the right) and SHEFFIELD PIKE (to the left).

Turn right and follow the path as it snakes up to the summit of GLENRIDDING DODD marked by a cairn on a rocky outcrop.

**ROUTE MAP: PATTERDALE TO HELVELLYN YH**

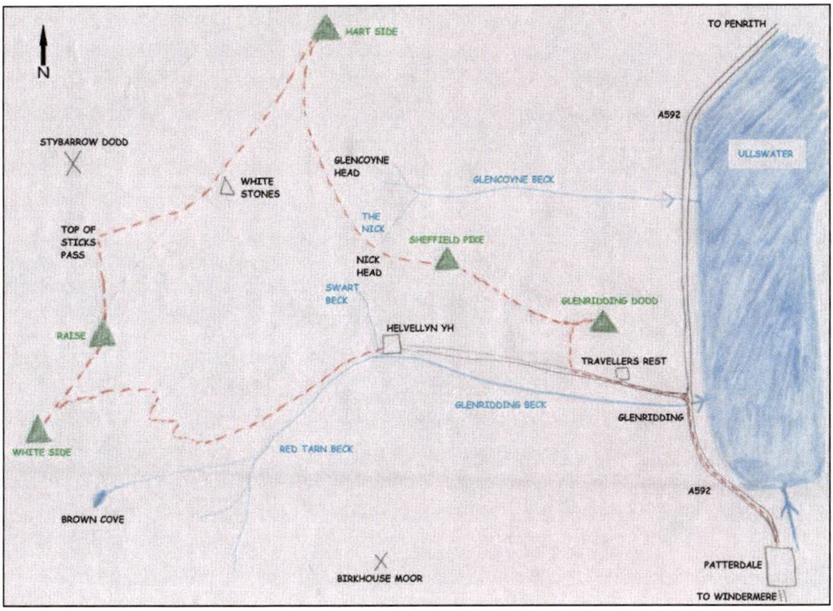


## GLENRIDDING DODD to SHEFFIELD PIKE

**1.5km (0.9 miles) distance - 280m (924 feet) ascent**

**Route:** Return to the col and cross it taking the path rising up the ridge on the other side. Cross the broken wall and continue up the path. Pass an old stone marker post with "H" on one side and "M" on the other. Stay on the path upwards.

When the crags are finished, there is a small cairn and a small stretch of level ground with a few small tarns. Cross this level ground and follow the path ahead up to summit cairn.

## SHEFFIELD PIKE to HART SIDE

**2.4km (1.5 miles) distance - 190m (627 feet) ascent**

**Route:** Take the path west down to the col at Nick Head. From the col, pick up the path bearing 310° up the ridge to the right of the old quarry scar. (Partway up notice a path cut across you – this will be tomorrow's path to Dockray.)

At the beginning of a steep section with some boulders to your left, the path forks and you should take the right-hand path. After the steep section, the path becomes intermittently faint, but follow it until a fork where you take the path heading at 330°.

After contouring above Glencoyne Head, the path forks and you take the left-hand path. As you reach a section of level ground, a path merges with yours from the left. (This is the path you will be taking as you come back from HART SIDE in a short while.) There is a short rise to the summit ahead, marked by the right-hand cairn of two beyond a ditch near the top.

## HART SIDE to RAISE

**2.8km (1.8 miles) distance - 175m (578 feet) ascent**

**Route:** Return the way you came until you reach the fork in the path that you came from earlier – bear right on the major path. Shortly afterwards, bear right at another fork to cross diagonally to the col between STYBARROW DODD and White Stones.

Just before the path reaches the main path on the col, bear left, cross the main path and continue down to reach the path running from White Stones to Sticks Pass. Turn right on this path to go to the top of Sticks Pass, marked by a cairn in the col between STYBARROW DODD and RAISE. *From there, head south-east up the clear path to RAISE, marked by an impressive, neat cairn.

## RAISE to WHITE SIDE

**1km (0.6 miles) distance - 45m (149 feet) ascent**

**Route:** Follow the path south-west from the summit marked by many cairns. Descend to the col and then make the short climb to WHITE SIDE with a wind-shelter at the summit.

## WHITE SIDE to Helvellyn YH

**3.6km (2.3 miles) distance - 0m (0 feet) ascent**

**Route:** Return down to the col then fork right, rising a little at first then levelling out before winding down to the valley bottom where you bear left to follow the valley down to the YH.

# Day 6

# Helvellyn YH to Troutbeck

**20.3km (12.7 miles) distance - 1130m (3729 feet) ascent - 630m (2079 feet) max altitude**

**Summary:** From Helvellyn YH, make the zig-zag climb up past Stang End to Lucy's Tongue and then return to the public footpath and continue to below the disused quarries above Nick Head. Take the public footpath that contours around Glencoyne Head and along the northern side of Glencoyne. Follow the path past Brown Hills, Swineside Knott and Common Fell all the way to Dockray. Cross the bridge on the A5091 and take the public footpath east down to cross Riddings Beck. Bear right and then follow up the southern side of the trees in the access land (there is a clear path) to the summit of GOWBARROW FELL. Continue round to the shooting lodge and take the public footpath through the trees at Swinburn's Park and over to the road near Underwood. A short stretch of road-walking takes you up to The Hause and a short, steep ascent takes you up LITTLE MELL FELL. Come back down to the road again and follow it, west then north, round to the little left-hand lane just after Brownrigg Farm. Follow the lane for a short way and then enter the access land and make the steady ascent up the broad ridge to the summit of GREAT MELL FELL. Carry on over and very steeply down to the disused rifle range which leads down to the A5091 and Troutbeck.

| MAPS | WAINWRIGHTS | M | FEET |
|---|---|---|---|
| OL5 | GOWBARROW FELL | 481 | 1587 |
| | LITTLE MELL FELL | 505 | 1667 |
| | GREAT MELL FELL | 537 | 1772 |

## Helvellyn YH to GOWBARROW FELL

**8.8km (5.5 miles) distance - 570m (1881 feet) ascent**

**Route:** Start back up the track you came down yesterday but follow signs for Sticks Pass which forks off right to climb the hillside in a zig-zag. After zig-zagging, the path swings over to Swart Beck and kicks sharply left to fork up the hillside at a small cairn near a ruined building on your right and just before a ruined building ahead.

When you reach a small dam at Lucy's Tongue, turn left up the hillside and cover a short pathless stretch to regain the main Sticks Pass path – turn right onto the path. Follow it to the footbridge, cross and follow the path (vaguely marked by cairns) as it arcs left at first through the old quarry and you reach a large flat expanse on your left.

Keep on the path until just before you reach the hillside ahead where you can pick up a faint path forking right to make its way over the shoulder, below the large quarry scar on the hillside towards Nick Head where you were yesterday.

(There is a confusing criss-cross of faint paths in this area, but so long as you keep in mind the aim of getting onto the path you crossed yesterday near Nick Head, then you can pick your own way there. You could alternatively have crossed the stream shortly after the Lucy's Tongue dam and made your way directly to Nick Head.)

Once you are on the path that you crossed yesterday, it drops over the shoulder to contour Glencoyne Head and along the northern side of Glencoyne. *Cross the stone stile in the wall and continue on the path. After a while, the path follows a wall. When the wall veers right downhill towards GOWBARROW FELL, leave the wall and stay on the path ahead.

Continue down and go through the gate to the right of the buildings onto the lane. At the end of the lane turn left and go over the bridge to the Royal Hotel in Dockray.**

Turn right and take the public footpath to the right of the post-box. Cross the river at the bottom and continue on the path. Go through the gate and turn left up to another gate. From here take the path up the hill to the trig point on GOWBARROW FELL.

**ROUTE MAP A: HELVELLYN YH TO DOCKRAY**

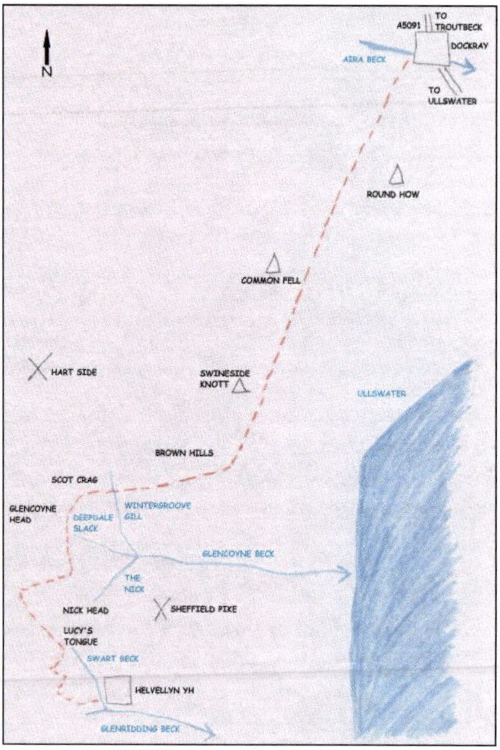

## ROUTE MAP B: DOCKRAY TO TROUTBECK

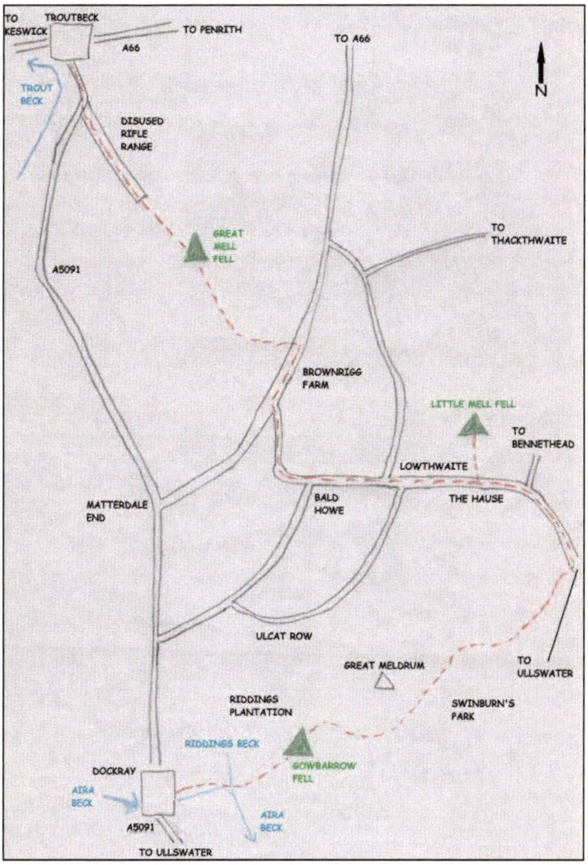


# GOWBARROW FELL to LITTLE MELL FELL

**4.6km (2.9 miles) distance - 260m (858 feet) ascent**

**Route:** Take the path heading north-east, which is rough at first, then becomes a good path and leads to a ruined building. Go through the gate on the left and into Swinburn's Park plantation. Follow the path to the other side of the plantation where you go through a gate.

Follow the path and then go over a stile on the left and continue on the path. Go through a gate and follow the path to the road. Turn left and walk up the road to the col with a layby on the left and take the public footpath on the right. Go up the permitted path to the trig point at the summit of LITTLE MELL FELL.

## LITTLE MELL FELL to GREAT MELL FELL

**5km (3.1 miles) distance - 300m (990 feet) ascent**

**Route:** Go back down to the road and turn right. Ignore a left turn, a right turn and another left turn. At the end of the road, turn right.

After passing Brownrigg Farm, go up the rough lane on the left. Ignore the 1st stile on the right and go over the 2nd. The path goes up to the left by the fence. As you emerge from the trees, take the right-hand path directly uphill. At the summit there is a small cairn.

## GREAT MELL FELL to Troutbeck

**1.9km (1.2 miles) distance - 0m (0 feet) ascent**

**Route:** Take the path at 330°. This is a faint path steeply down to the disused rifle range. Enter the range through the gate on its left-hand side and walk down the range to the road at the bottom (A5091). Turn right for Troutbeck which is just a few minutes along the road, almost at the A66.

# Day7

# Troutbeck to Helvellyn YH

**20.6km (12.9miles) distance - 870m (2871 feet) ascent - 857m (2828 feet) max altitude**

**Summary:** From Troutbeck, a stretch of road-walking on the A5091 takes you to Binks Moss and you turn right onto "New Road", which you take past Cockley Moor to the junction at Red Moss. Turn right onto the Old Coach Road which you follow between Wolfcrag Moss and Barbaryrigg Moss and over Mariel Bridge. Head up the ridge of White Pike but pass to the south of the crags to reach the north-east ridge of CLOUGH HEAD which you follow to the summit. You then head down towards Calfhow Pike, but cut the corner to swing up the ridge to GREAT DODD. A pleasant ridge walk takes you onto WATSON'S DODD. An easy climb takes you onto STYBARROW DODD, from where, head down to the top of Sticks Pass and take the public footpath east down to Helvellyn YH.

## Troutbeck to CLOUGH HEAD

**11.7km (7.3 miles) distance - 530m (1749 feet) ascent**

**Route:** Walk back down the A5091 past the rifle range and turn right when signposted for High

Row and Dowthwaite Head. At the T-junction where there is a rough car-park, turn right onto the public footpath for St John's in the Vale which is the "Old Coach Road".*

Follow this path and, after crossing the stream (either at the ford or over the footbridge), stay on the main track ahead. Go through a gate and over Mosedale Beck on Mariel Bridge.

Ignore the immediate stile on the left and take the 2nd. Follow the faint path up to the left of White Pike. Once you are behind White Pike, the path is clear and goes up to the trig point and small wind-shelter on the summit of CLOUGH HEAD.

## ROUTE MAP A: TROUTBECK TO GREAT DODD

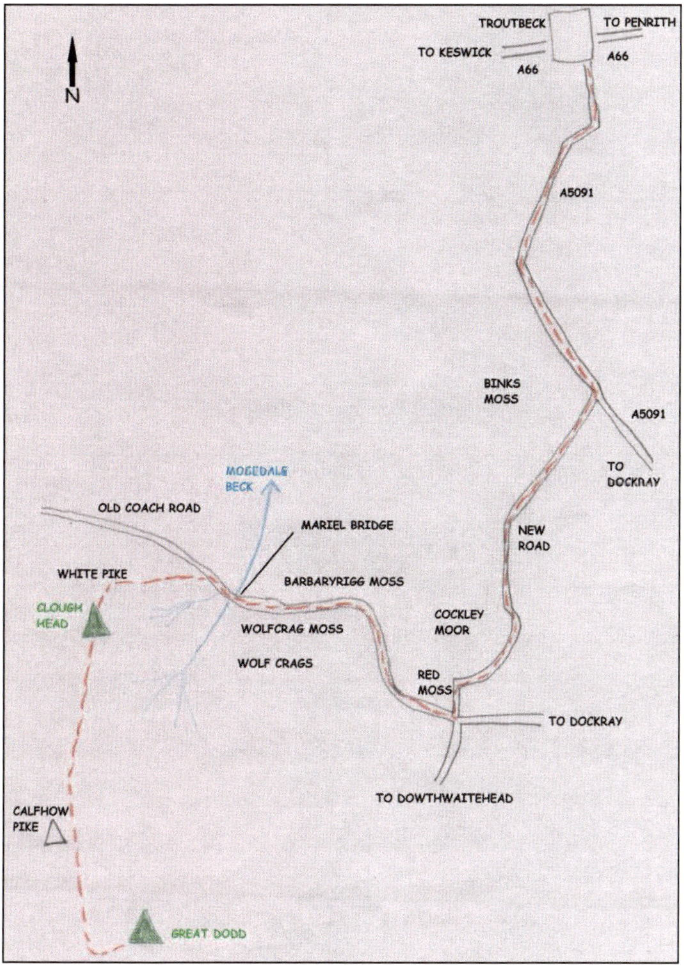

## ROUTE MAP B: GREAT DODD TO HELVELLYN YH

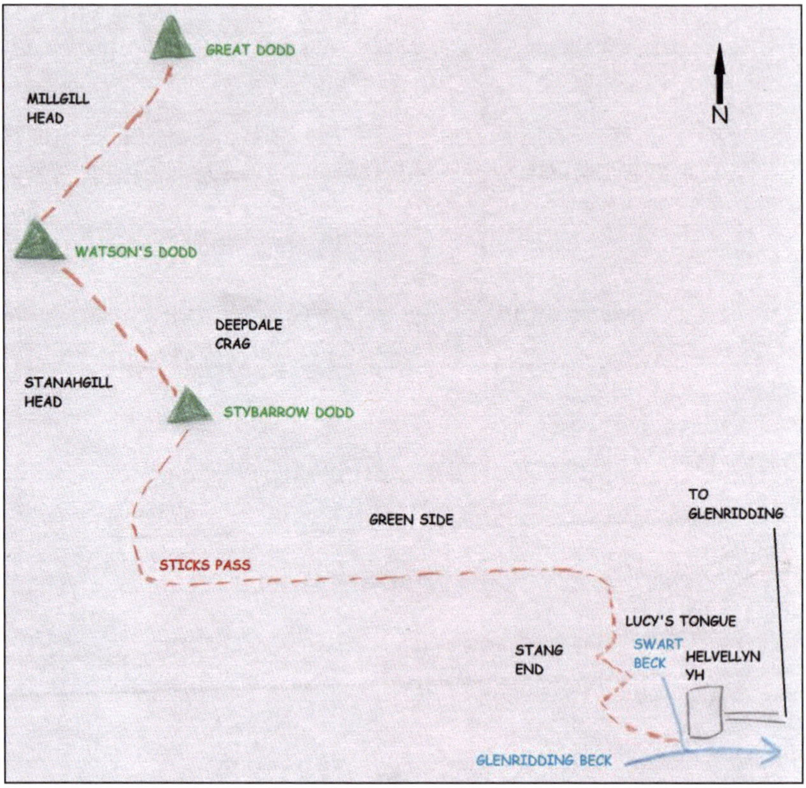


| MAPS | WAINWRIGHTS | M | FEET |
|---|---|---|---|
| OL5 | CLOUGH HEAD | 726 | 2396 |
| | GREAT DODD | 857 | 2828 |
| | WATSON'S DODD | 789 | 2604 |
| | STYBARROW DODD | 843 | 2782 |

## CLOUGH HEAD to GREAT DODD

**2.6km (1.6 miles) distance - 250m (825 feet) ascent**

**Route:** Take the 210° path to drop to the col then climb up the other side but bear left to bypass Calfhow Pike and follow the path up the ridge as it arcs right to left onto the summit of GREAT DODD marked by a cairn with a shelter to the south-east.

## GREAT DODD to WATSON'S DODD

**1.3km (0.8 miles) distance - 15m (50 feet) ascent**

**Route:** Go over to the shelter and then head at 200° to pick up the path down the ridge. After the ridge, take the right fork for a gentle rise to the summit cairn on WATSON'S DODD.

## WATSON'S DODD to STYBARROW DODD

**1km (0.6 miles) distance - 75m (248 feet) ascent**

**Route:** Take the 110° path to rejoin the main GREAT DODD to STYBARROW DODD path where you turn right and climb. The path bypasses the summit, (don't mistakenly think the summit is marked by the cairn on the south-western spur of STYBARROW DODD which is visible from the main path),so, after the climb, when the path is almost level, turn sharp left for a short final climb to the summit marked by a cairn with a slate sticking out of it. To the south-east of the cairn are a shelter and an old wall.

## STYBARROW DODD to Helvellyn YH

**4km (2.5 miles) distance - 0m (0 feet) ascent**

**Route:** Go 210° to rejoin the main path to the south-western spur, which then swings left down to the col at the top of Sticks Pass.** Turn left and go down Sticks Pass and after a while you will be back in the disused quarry workings at the end of the flat expanse of ground from yesterday.

Bear right to find the little footbridge and then follow the cairn-marked Sticks Pass path back down to Helvellyn YH.

## Day 8

## Helvellyn YH to Patterdale

**11.5km (7.2 miles) distance - 870m (2871 feet) ascent - 950m (3135 feet) max altitude**

**Summary:** From Helvellyn YH, follow the public footpath up the southern side of Glenridding Beck and up the western side of Red Tarn Beck but leave the path to climb the eastern ridge (to the south of the crags) of CATSTYE CAM. Follow the ridge down and up Swirral Edge onto HELVELLYN, the highest fell of the week. Follow the ridge south to NETHERMOST PIKE and then come back almost all the way to HELVELLYN but go down Striding Edge and past Hole-in-the-Wall to BIRKHOUSE MOOR (the summit of which is near the wall-corner). From there, you head east, then take the public footpath that goes south-west through the wall and pick up the public footpath that heads eastwards to the bottom of Brownend Plantation. Take the public footpath south-east across Grisedale Beck and head north-east on the tarmacked road to the A592 at Grisedale Bridge. Turn right and complete the day with a short road-walk into Patterdale for another overnight stay there.

### ROUTE MAP: HELVELLYN YH TO PATTERDALE

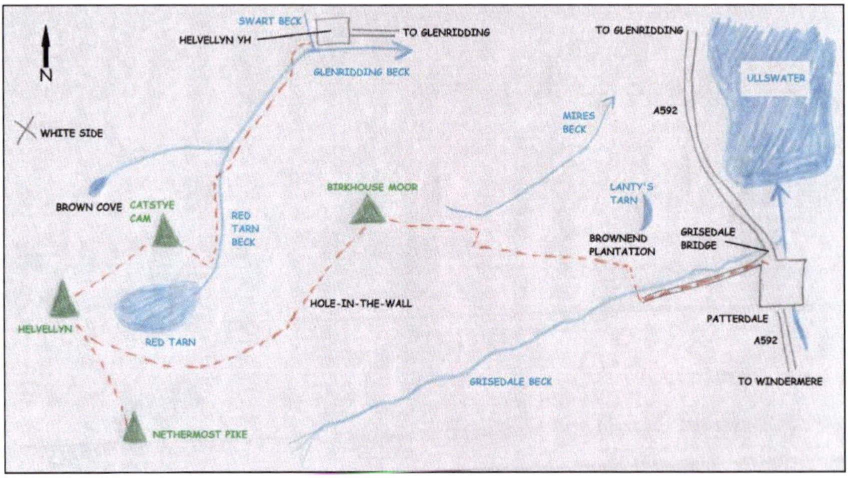


| MAPS | WAINWRIGHTS | M | FEET |
|---|---|---|---|
| OL5 | CATSTYE CAM | 890 | 2937 |
| | HELVELLYN | 950 | 3135 |
| | NETHERMOST PIKE | 891 | 2940 |
| | BIRKHOUSE MOOR | 718 | 2369 |

## Helvellyn YH to CATSTYE CAM

**3.1km (1.9 miles) distance - 610m (2013 feet) ascent**

**Route:** Go back up the track you came down yesterday but follow the sign for Red Tarn and Helvellyn. Cross the bridge and continue up the path. Just before the gradient lessens for the approach to Red Tarn, turn right (no path) to pick up the path ascending the eastern ridge to the obvious pinnacle summit of CATSTYE CAM marked by a cairn.

## CATSTYE CAM to HELVELLYN

**1km (0.6 miles) distance - 130m (429 feet) ascent**

**Route:** Follow the south-western path down to the col and up Swirral Edge. At the top, turn left and go past the trig point to find the summit cairn and just beyond it a wind shelter.

## HELVELLYN to NETHERMOST PIKE

**1km (0.6 miles) distance - 30m (99 feet) ascent**

**Route:** Follow the path south from the shelter to a col and then bear left up to NETHERMOST PIKE marked by the 2nd cairn. There are also a 3rd cairn and a shelter a little further on.

## NETHERMOST PIKE to BIRKHOUSE MOOR

**3km (1.9 miles) distance - 100m (330 feet) ascent**

**Route:** Head back to Helvellyn, but follow the edge on your right and, just before the summit, take the unpleasant path steeply down to Striding Edge from near the monument. Take the crest of Striding Edge or the side-path and continue to Hole-in-the-Wall, but don't cross the wall.

The path along the north-western side of the wall leads to BIRKHOUSE MOOR which is marked by a cairn just before the wall turns east. (There is a cairn further on for good views, but that is not the summit.)

## BIRKHOUSE MOOR to Patterdale

**3.4km (2.1 miles) distance - 0m (0 feet) ascent**

**Route:** Follow the wall as it swings east downhill. Join the major path coming from your left (from the further cairn of BIRKHOUSE MOOR). When the main path swings left at a cairn to follow down Mires Beck, leave the main path by continuing straight on. When the ground levels out, turn right and go over the stone stile in the wall.

Follow the faint path ahead then turn left on the faint path that soon cuts across you. Follow this path diagonally down and cross the fence at the stile. Continue diagonally downwards on the path, go past the corner of the fence and after the ground levels out, a path cuts back on the right to drop down to the main path lower down. Turn left and go down to another path coming across you level.

Go through the gate and straight down to the track ahead through a gate. Cross the bridge and either follow the road down to the main road (A592) or turn right to find the first of 3 possible footpaths that can take you over the shoulder and bring you into Patterdale on the same path that you came in on after ARNISON CRAG on Day 4. The other 2 footpaths that can do this are further down the tarmac road that leads to the A592.

## Day 9

## Patterdale to Ambleside

**15.5km (9.7 miles) distance - 845m (2789 feet) ascent - 873m (2881 feet) max altitude**

**Summary:** From Patterdale, head south on the A592 to Deepdale Bridge and then climb the ridge over HARTSOP-ABOVE-HOW onto HART CRAG. Follow the ridge north-west over Link Hause and swing past Flinty Grave to the summit of FAIRFIELD. From there, descend the ridge over GREAT RIGG, HERON PIKE and NAB SCAR to emerge from the fells at Rydal Hall. Go back through the grounds of the Hall and Rydal Park to Scandale Bridge and follow the A591 back to Ambleside and congratulate yourself on having bagged all 35 Wainwrights in The Eastern Fells!

### ROUTE MAP A: PATTERDALE TO FAIRFIELD

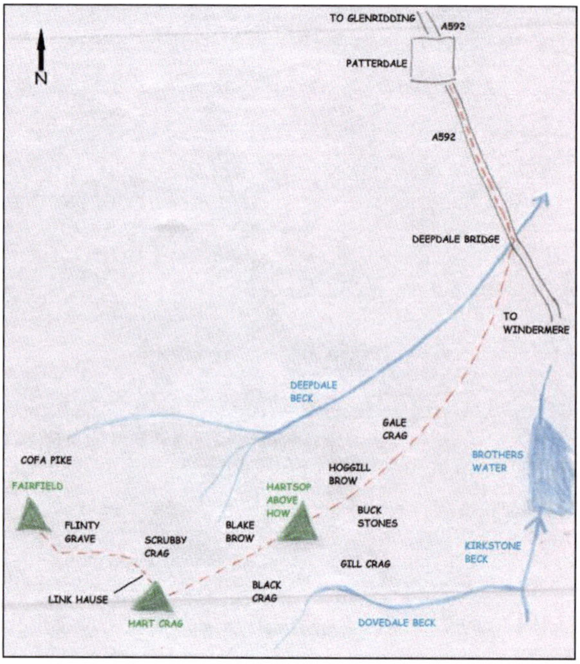

## ROUTE MAP B: FAIRFIELD TO AMBLESIDE

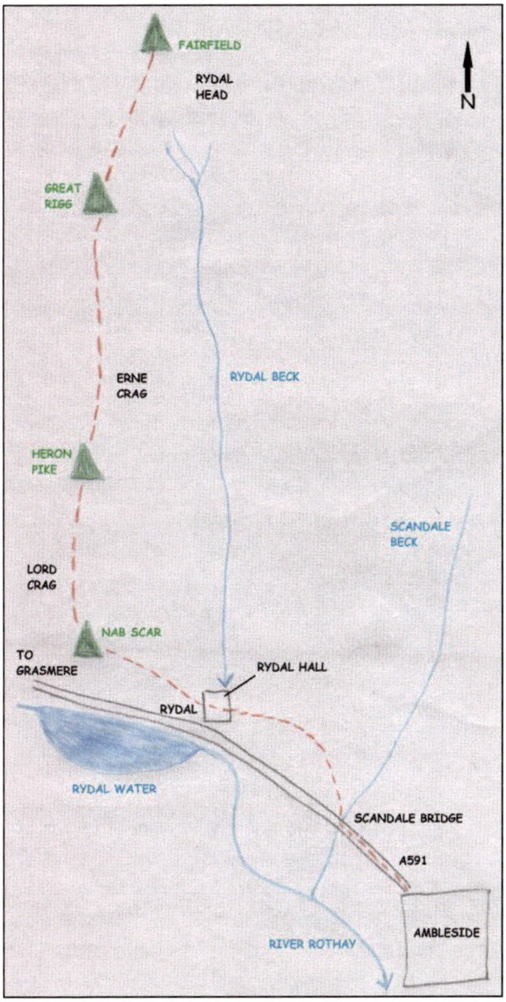


| MAPS | WAINWRIGHTS | M | FEET |
|---|---|---|---|
| OL5, OL7 | HARTSOP-ABOVE-HOW | 580 | 1914 |
| | HART CRAG | 822 | 2713 |
| | FAIRFIELD | 873 | 2881 |
| | GREAT RIGG | 766 | 2528 |
| | HERON PIKE | 612 | 2020 |
| | NAB SCAR | 440 | 1452 |

## Patterdale to HARTSOP-ABOVE-HOW

**4.4km (2.8 miles) distance - 425m (1403 feet) ascent**

**Route:** Walk south on the A592 and just after the double bridge (Deepdale Bridge), when you have crossed the river, take the public footpath to the right at the bus stop just after the old phone box. Follow the marker posts up the track and then left to the gate in the fence.

Stay on the path through the trees, go through a gate and follow the marker post ahead. The path follows the wall up the ridge. Cross the stile over the cross-wall and continue up the ridge. Ignore a ladder-stile on the left. Eventually the wall drops away to the left downhill, but the path continues up the ridge. The summit of HARTSOP-ABOVE-HOW is a rocky knoll without a cairn above Gill Crag.

## HARTSOP-ABOVE-HOW to HART CRAG

**1.8km (1.1 miles) distance - 250m (825 feet) ascent**

**Route:** Continue down to a col and along the ridge. For the final climb, the path splits either side of some crags ahead – take the left-hand route for an easier climb up a shallow gully. The summit is confusing in mist. The highest point is marked by a cairn at the south-eastern end of the summit.

## HART CRAG to FAIRFIELD

**1.2km (0.8 miles) distance - 100m (330 feet) ascent**

**Route:** The path goes north-west down to the col and then steeply up the other side. After the steep section, the cairned path swings west then bears north around Flinty Grave to reach the summit cairn beyond a couple of shelters.

## FAIRFIELD to GREAT RIGG

**1.4km (0.9 miles) distance - 30m (99 feet) ascent**

**Route:** From the shelters, go 200$^{\circ}$ to pick up the path down the ridge to GREAT RIGG which is reached after a slight rise and is marked by a cairn.

## GREAT RIGG to HERON PIKE

**2.2km (1.4 miles) distance - 40m (132 feet) ascent**

**Route:** Continue down the ridge. At the cairn, take the left-hand path staying on the ridge (the right-hand path goes down the other ridge to STONE ARTHUR). Go past a tarn and then either over or past Erne Crag, to a col and up to the cairnless summit of HERON PIKE.

*Nab Scar and Heron Pike from Rydal Park*

## HERON PIKE to NAB SCAR

**1km (0.6 miles) distance - 0m (0 feet) ascent**

**Route:** Continue on the path down the ridge. After a while it follows a collapsed wall which leads to a cairn on the right near a stone stile in a wall ahead. This cairn marks the summit.

## NAB SCAR to Ambleside

**3.5km (2.2 miles) distance - 0m (0 feet) ascent**

**Route:** Go over the stone stile and continue down the path. Go over a stile and then through a gate at the bottom. Go down the concrete track to the tarmac road to Rydal Hall.

Go through the Rydal Hall complex and back along the path to Ambleside that you came along the other way on Day 3.

# DOCKRAY 9-DAY ITINERARY

## SUMMARY

**Days 1 to 4** are the same as for the Standard 9-Day Itinerary (pg 30). 13 Wainwrights done.

**Day 5** takes you over GLENRIDDING DODD, SHEFFIELD PIKE and HART SIDE before dropping you into the hamlet of Dockray for an overnight stay. 16 Wainwrights done.

**Day 6** is a circular walk tackling GOWBARROW FELL, LITTLE MELL FELL and GREAT MELL FELL before returning for a second consecutive night in Dockray. 19 Wainwrights done.

**Day 7** covers CLOUGH HEAD, GREAT DODD, WATSON'S DODD, STYBARROW DODD, RAISE and WHITE SIDE before dropping to Helvellyn YH for the night. 25 Wainwrights done.

**Days 8 & 9** are the same as for the Standard 9-Day Itinerary (pg 30). 35 Wainwrights done!!!

*Windermere from High Pike*

## Days 1 to 4

## Ambleside to Patterdale

Follow Standard 9-Day Itinerary, Days 1 to 4 (pg 33-44).

## ITINERARY MAP: DOCKRAY 9-DAY ITINERARY

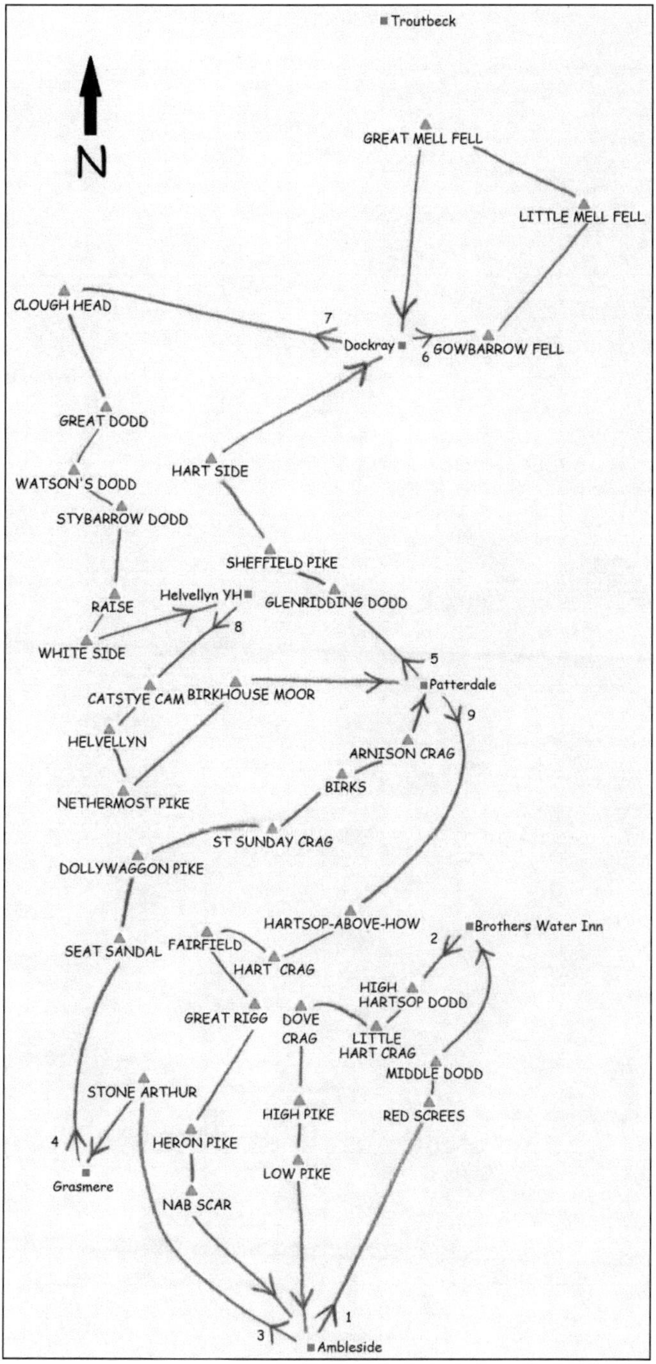

## DISTANCES, ASCENTS AND MAXIMUM ALTITUDES:

### DOCKRAY 9-DAY ITINERARY

| DAY | FROM | TO | DISTANCE | | ASCENT | | MAX ALTITUDE | |
|---|---|---|---|---|---|---|---|---|
| | | | KM | MILES | M | FEET | M | FEET |
| 1 | AMBLESIDE | BROTHERS WATER INN | 9.8 | 6.1 | 745 | 2459 | 776 | 2561 |
| 2 | BROTHERS WATER INN | AMBLESIDE | 10.7 | 6.7 | 705 | 2327 | 792 | 2614 |
| 3 | AMBLESIDE | GRASMERE | 9.9 | 6.2 | 500 | 1650 | 500 | 1650 |
| 4 | GRASMERE | PATTERDALE | 14.3 | 8.9 | 1355 | 4472 | 858 | 2831 |
| 5 | PATTERDALE | DOCKRAY | 12 | 7.5 | 770 | 2541 | 756 | 2495 |
| 6 | DOCKRAY | DOCKRAY | 17.6 | 11 | 830 | 2739 | 537 | 1772 |
| 7 | DOCKRAY | HELVELLYN YH | 17 | 10.6 | 1020 | 3366 | 883 | 2914 |
| 8 | HELVELLYN YH | PATTERDALE | 11.5 | 7.2 | 870 | 2871 | 950 | 3135 |
| 9 | PATTERDALE | AMBLESIDE | 15.5 | 9.7 | 845 | 2789 | 873 | 2881 |
| | | **TOTALS** | **118.3** | **73.9** | **7640** | **25212** | | |

# Day 5

## Patterndale to Dockray

**12km (7.5 miles) distance - 770m (2541 feet) ascent - 756m (2495 feet) max altitude**

**Summary:** From Patterdale, a short stretch of road-walking north on the A592 takes you to Glenridding and just after Glenridding Bridge you turn left up the road past the Travellers Rest pub to the foot of Blaes Crag. You ascend The Rake north to the wall and then a short return journey to the east ticks off GLENRIDDING DODD. From The Rake, you now head north-west over Heron pike to SHEFFIELD PIKE. You now drop to Nick Head and then climb to the east of the disused quarries to head north above Glencoyne Head. This leads you across the col to the summit of HART SIDE. Head over the col and rising ground to the south-east and follow the wall down to pick up the public footpath that passes Brown Hills, Swineside Knott and Common Fell all the way to Dockray.

### ROUTE MAP: PATTERDALE TO DOCKRAY

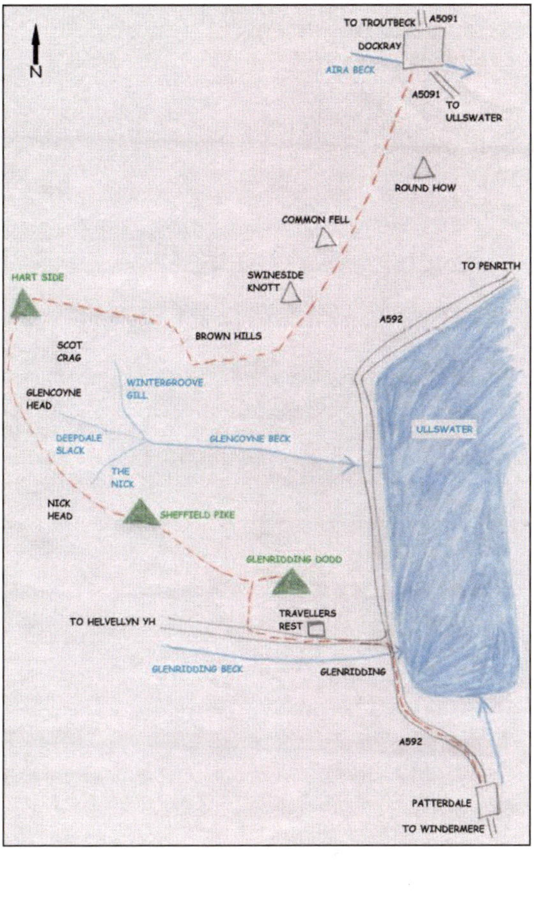

| MAPS | WAINWRIGHTS | M | FEET |
|---|---|---|---|
| OL5 | GLENRIDDING DODD | 442 | 1459 |
| | SHEFFIELD PIKE | 675 | 2228 |
| | HART SIDE | 756 | 2495 |

Follow Standard 9-Day Itinerary, Day 5 as far as HART SIDE (pg 44 - 46).

## HART SIDE to Dockray path

**1.4km (0.9 mile) distance - 10m (33 feet) ascent**

**Route:** Leave the summit at 110° and, after a short descent, take the right-hand path over the rising ground ahead. Cross the small, flat top and descend on the same bearing to the wall. Turn right and follow the wall down. Ignore the first 2 stiles (wooden) in the wall and then you reach the path for Dockray coming across you at the stone stile in the wall.

## Dockray Path to Dockray

**3.3km (2.1 mile) distance - 0m (0 feet) ascent**

Follow Standard 9-Day Itinerary, Day 6 from * to ** (pg 48).

## Day 6

## Dockray to Dockray

**17.6km (11 miles) distance - 830m (2739 feet) ascent - 537m (1772 feet) max altitude**

**Summary:** Take the public footpath east down to cross Riddings Beck. Bear right and then follow up the southern side of the trees in the access land (there is a clear path) to the summit of GOWBARROW FELL. Continue round to the shooting lodge and take the public footpath through the trees at Swinburn's Park and over to the road near Underwood. A short stretch of road-walking takes you up to The Hause and a short, steep ascent takes you up LITTLE MELL FELL. Come back down to the road again and follow it, west then north, round to the little left-hand lane just after Brownrigg Farm. Follow the lane for a short way and then enter the access land and make the steady ascent up the broad ridge to the summit of GREAT MELL FELL. You then turn back and come down the same way to the road. Walk the road south back past Brownrigg Farm, bear left, turn right at Bald Howe and turn left for Ulcat Row. Where the road bends left, just before Ulcat Row, take the public footpath that leads below Norman Crag back to Riddings Beck near Millses and then head back up into Dockray for a second consecutive night's stay.

**ROUTE MAP: DOCKRAY TO DOCKRAY**

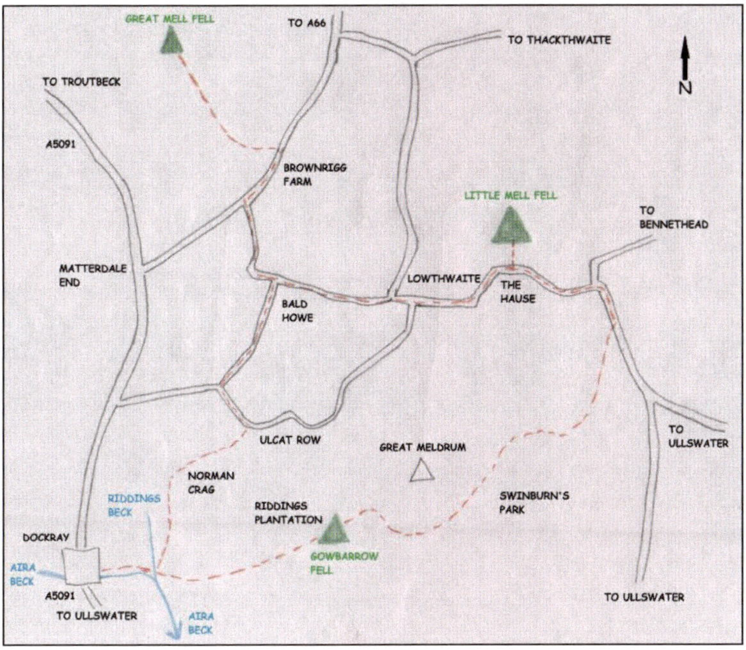


| MAPS | WAINWRIGHTS | M | FEET |
|---|---|---|---|
| OL5 | GOWBARROW FELL | 481 | 1587 |
| | LITTLE MELL FELL | 505 | 1667 |
| | GREAT MELL FELL | 537 | 1772 |

## Dockray to GREAT MELL FELL

**11.3km (7.1 mile) distance - 760m (2508 feet) ascent**

Follow Standard 9-Day Itinerary, Day 6 from ** to GREAT MELL FELL (pg 48 - 50).

## GREAT MELL FELL to Dockray

**6.3km (3.9 miles) distance - 70m (231 feet) ascent**

**Route:** Go back down GREAT MELL FELL the way you came up and go back down the lane to the road. Go back along the road past Brownrigg Farm. Take the left hand turn signposted 'Dockray 2'. Cross a little stream, ignore the footpath to the right on the left hand bend. Take the right turn signposted 'Ulcat Row ¾'. Take the left turn signed 'Ulcat Row'. When you reach the cottages named 'Undercragg' on your left at a left-hand bend, take the public footpath on your right signposted for 'Dockray 1 mile' through the gate. When you reach the river, you are back at the bottom of GOWBARROW FELL, turn right, cross the bridge and climb back up to Dockray.

## Day 7

## Dockray to Helvellyn YH

**17km (10.6 miles) distance - 1020m (3366 feet) ascent - 883m (2914 feet) max altitude**

**Summary:** A short stretch of road-walking east takes you up to the junction at Red Moss. Continue straight onto the Old Coach Road which you follow between Wolfcrag Moss and Barbaryrigg Moss and over Mariel Bridge. Head up the ridge of White Pike but pass to the south of the crags to reach the north-east ridge of CLOUGH HEAD which you follow to the summit. You then head down towards Calfhow Pike, but cut the corner to swing up the ridge to GREAT DODD. A pleasant ridge walk takes you onto WATSON'S DODD. An easy climb takes you onto STYBARROW DODD, from where, head down to the top of Sticks Pass. Make the steady climb south to RAISE. From there, descend and climb south-west to WHITE SIDE (marked as Whiteside Bank) before turning back briefly and turning down to zig-zag down into Glenridding valley and follow down to Helvellyn YH.

| MAPS | WAINWRIGHTS | M | FEET |
|---|---|---|---|
| OL5 | CLOUGH HEAD | 726 | 2396 |
| | GREAT DODD | 857 | 2828 |
| | WATSON'S DODD | 789 | 2604 |
| | STYBARROW DODD | 843 | 2782 |
| | RAISE | 883 | 2914 |
| | WHITE SIDE | 863 | 2848 |

### Dockray to 'Old Coach Road'

**1.4km (0.9 miles) distance - 120m (396 feet) ascent**

**Route:** From the Royal Hotel, climb the road sign-posted for 'Dowthwaite Head 2 miles'. Ignore footpaths off to the right and left and stay on the road to the T-junction and rough car-park shortly after Cockley Moor Cottage.

## ROUTE MAP A: DOCKRAY TO WATSON'S DODD

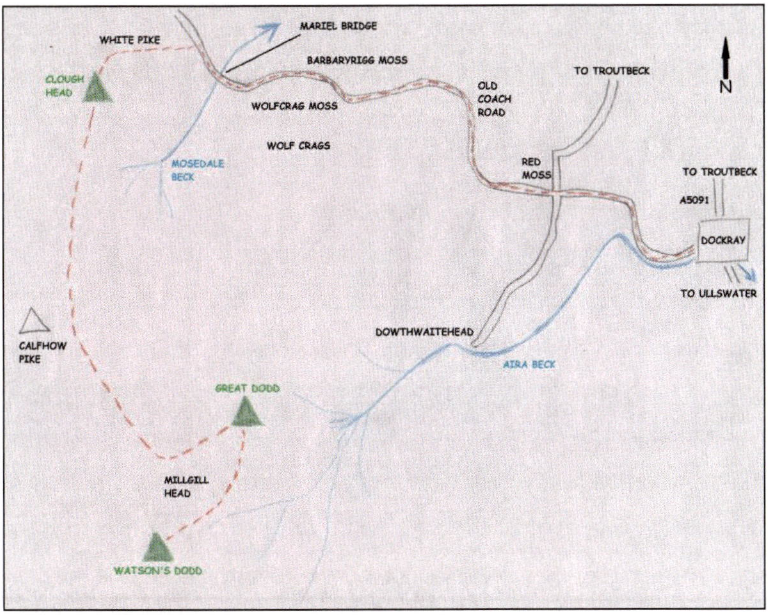


## ROUTE MAP B: WATSON'S DODD TO HELVELLYN YH

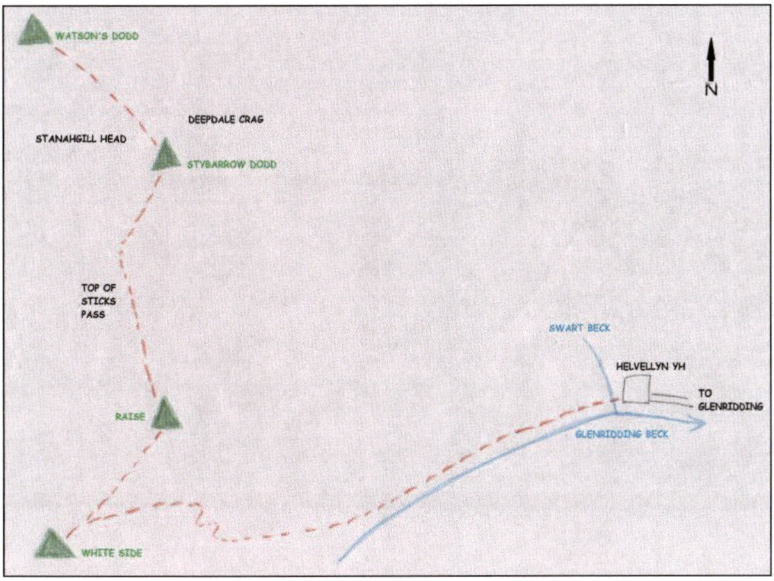

## 'Old Coach Road' to Top of Sticks Pass

**10.3km (6.4 miles) distance - 715m (2360 feet) ascent**

Follow Standard 9-Day Itinerary, Day 7 from * to ** (pg 51 - 53).

## Top of Sticks Pass to Helvellyn YH

**5.3km (3.3 miles) distance - 185m (611 feet) ascent**

Follow Standard 9-Day Itinerary, Day 5 from * to Helvellyn YH (pg 46).

## Days 8 to 9

## Helvellyn YH to Ambleside

Follow Standard 9-Day Itinerary, Days 8 to 9 (pg 53 - 59).

*Grasmere from the base of Seat Sandal*

# EDGES 9-DAY ITINERARY

## SUMMARY

**Days 1 to 3** are the same as for the Standard 9-Day Itinerary (pg 30). 8 Wainwrights done.

**Day 4** takes you over SEAT SANDAL, ST SUNDAY CRAG, BIRKS and ARNISON CRAG to Patterdale. 12 Wainwrights done.

**Days 5 & 6** are the same as for the Dockray 9-Day Itinerary (pg 60). 18 Wainwrights done.

**Day 7** tackles CLOUGH HEAD, GREAT DODD, WATSON'S DODD, STYBARROW DODD, RAISE and WHITE SIDE before dropping past Helvellyn YH to Patterdale for the night. 24 Wainwrights done.

**Day 8** is a circular walk from Patterdale taking you up BIRKHOUSE MOOR, CATSTYE CAM, HELVELLYN via Swirral Edge, NETHERMOST PIKE and DOLLYWAGGON PIKE and returning down Grisedale. 29 Wainwrights done.

**Day 9** is the same as for the Standard 9-Day Itinerary (pg 30). 35 Wainwrights done!!!

## Days 1 to 3

## Ambleside to Grasmere

Follow Standard 9-Day Itinerary, Days 1 to 3 (pg 33 - 40).

## Day 4

## Grasmere to Patterdale

**12.6km (7.9 miles) distance - 1075m (3548 feet) ascent - 841m (2775 feet) max altitude**

**Summary:** From Grasmere, a short road-walk up Easedale Rd and north past Thorny How hostel takes you to Mill Bridge on the A591, from where, you initially use the public bridleway until about the 170m contour and then climb the shoulder of SEAT SANDAL. From there, you drop steeply north to a col near Grisedale Tarn. You walk beside the tarn to its eastern end and you make an ascent up the flank and ridge of ST SUNDAY CRAG via Deepdale Hause. A steep descent and a gently undulating ascent take you to BIRKS. A steep descent leads you east to Trough Head, then, a final ascent for the day brings you to ARNISON CRAG. You descend by the wall north past Oxford Crag and follow the public footpath east into Patterdale for the night.

## ITINERARY MAP: EDGES 9-DAY ITINERARY

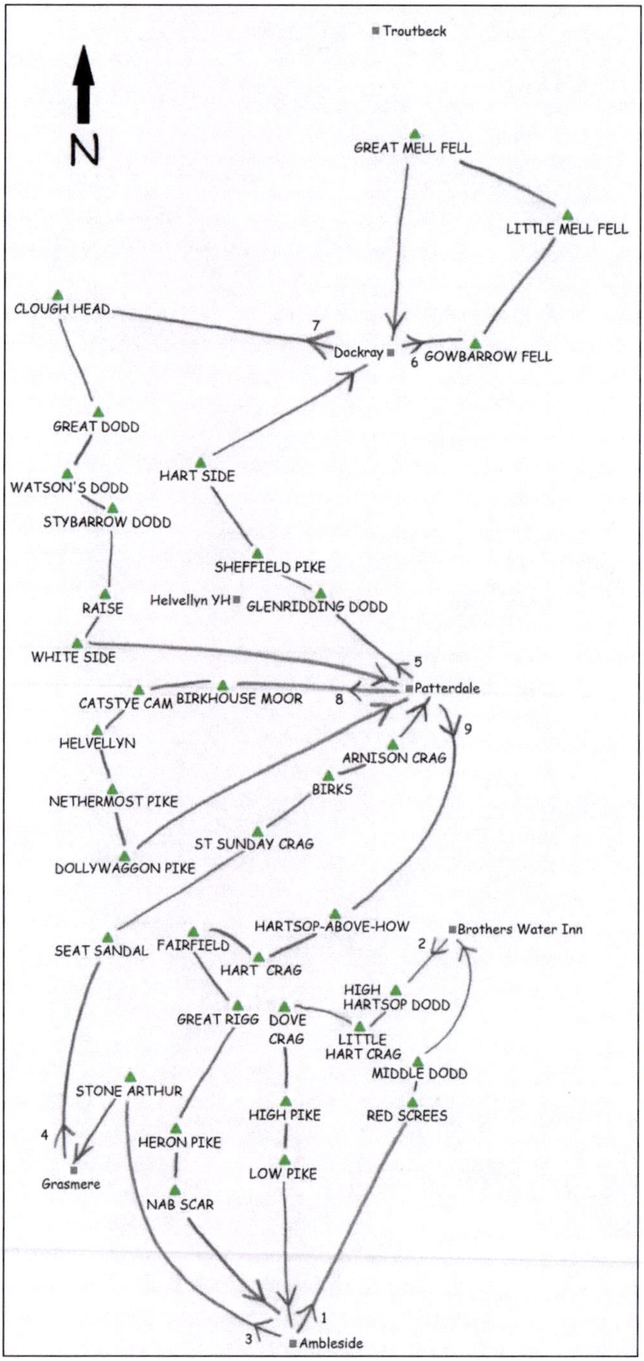

## DISTANCES, ASCENTS AND MAXIMUM ALTITUDES:

### EDGES 9-DAY ITINERARY

| DAY | FROM | TO | DISTANCE | | ASCENT | | MAX ALTITUDE | |
|---|---|---|---|---|---|---|---|---|
| | | | KM | MILES | M | FEET | M | FEET |
| 1 | AMBLESIDE | BROTHERS WATER INN | 9.8 | 6.1 | 745 | 2459 | 776 | 2561 |
| 2 | BROTHERS WATER INN | AMBLESIDE | 10.7 | 6.7 | 705 | 2327 | 792 | 2614 |
| 3 | AMBLESIDE | GRASMERE | 9.9 | 6.2 | 500 | 1650 | 500 | 1650 |
| 4 | GRASMERE | PATTERDALE | 12.6 | 7.9 | 1075 | 3548 | 841 | 2775 |
| 5 | PATTERDALE | DOCKRAY | 12 | 7.5 | 770 | 2541 | 756 | 2495 |
| 6 | DOCKRAY | DOCKRAY | 17.6 | 11 | 830 | 2739 | 537 | 1772 |
| 7 | DOCKRAY | PATTERDALE | 21.1 | 13.2 | 1020 | 3366 | 883 | 2914 |
| 8 | PATTERDALE | PATTERDALE | 17.9 | 11.2 | 1000 | 3300 | 950 | 3135 |
| 9 | PATTERDALE | AMBLESIDE | 15.5 | 9.7 | 845 | 2789 | 873 | 2881 |
| | | **TOTALS** | **127.1** | **79.4** | **7490** | **24717** | | |

## ROUTE MAP: GRASMERE TO PATTERDALE

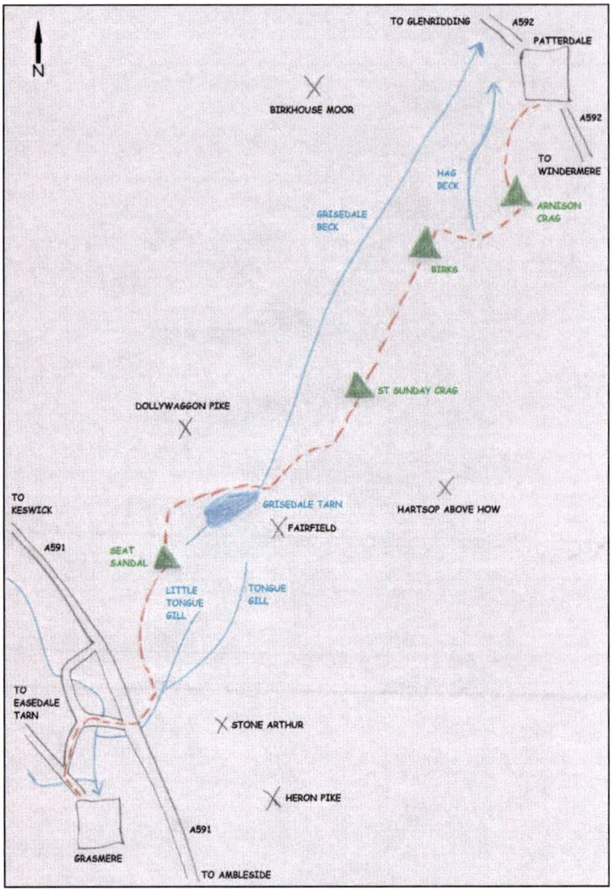


| MAPS | WAINWRIGHTS | M | FEET |
|---|---|---|---|
| OL5, OL7 | SEAT SANDAL | 736 | 2429 |
| | ST SUNDAY CRAG | 841 | 2775 |
| | BIRKS | 622 | 2053 |
| | ARNISON CRAG | 433 | 1429 |

## Grasmere to col

**5.1km (3.2 miles) distance - 710m (2343 feet) ascent**

Follow Standard 9-Day Itinerary, Day 4 to * (pg 41 - 42).

## Col to Patterdale

**7.5km (4.7 miles) distance - 365m (1205 feet) ascent**

**Route:** Turn right onto the path. Then bear left to follow the path along the left-hand side of the tarn (initially on the edge of the steep bank down to the tarn on your right). If you find yourself climbing away from the tarn, turn right and descend towards the tarn until you pick up the path and turn left. At the end of the tarn, a path comes across in front of you.

Follow Standard 9-Day Itinerary, Day 4 from ** to Patterdale (pg 43 - 44).

# Days 5 to 6

## Patterdale to Dockray

Follow Dockray 9-Day Itinerary, Days 5 to 6 (pg 63 - 66).

# Day 7

## Dockray to Patterdale

**21.1km (13.2 miles) distance - 1020m (3366 feet) ascent - 883m (2914 feet) max altitude**

**Summary:** A short stretch of road-walking west takes you up to the junction at Red Moss. Continue straight onto the Old Coach Road which you follow between Wolfcrag Moss and Barbaryrigg Moss and over Mariel Bridge. Head up the ridge of White Pike but pass to the south of the crags to reach the north-east ridge of CLOUGH HEAD which you follow to the summit. You then head down towards Calfhow Pike, but cut the corner to swing up the ridge to GREAT DODD. A pleasant ridge walk takes you onto WATSON'S DODD. An easy climb takes you onto STYBARROW DODD, from where, head down to the top of Sticks Pass. Make the steady climb south to RAISE. From there, descend and climb south-west to WHITE SIDE (marked as Whiteside Bank) before turning back briefly and turning down to zig-zag down into Glenridding valley and follow down past Helvellyn YH, down past Rake Cottages, past the Travellers rest pub and to the A592. Turn right and walk along the road to Patterdale.

Refer to 'ROUTE MAP A: DOCKRAY TO WATSON'S DODD' of Dockray 9-Day Itinerary, Day 7 (pg 67).

## ROUTE MAP B: WATSON'S DODD TO PATTERDALE

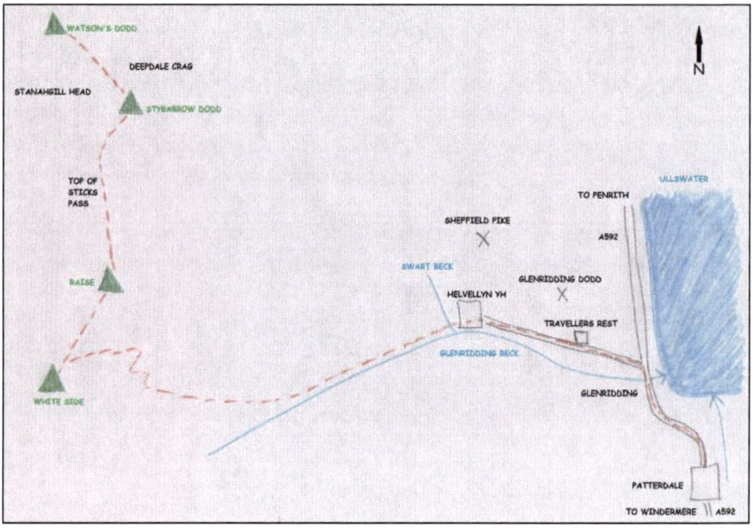


| MAPS | WAINWRIGHTS | M | FEET |
|---|---|---|---|
| OL5 | CLOUGH HEAD | 726 | 2396 |
| | GREAT DODD | 857 | 2828 |
| | WATSON'S DODD | 789 | 2604 |
| | STYBARROW DODD | 843 | 2782 |
| | RAISE | 883 | 2914 |
| | WHITE SIDE | 863 | 2848 |

Follow Dockray 9-Day Itinerary, Day 7 (pg 66 - 68).

## Helvellyn YH to Patterdale

**4.1km (2.6 miles) distance - 0m (0 feet) ascent**

**Route:** From the hostel, continue on down the track. It has stretches of rough stones and stretches of surfaced strips for car tyres. Ignore the footpath to the right signposted for Gillside to avoid any more climbing and especially if you have changed into your trainers. After the cattle grid and the houses, just keep following the road down, all the way past the Travellers Rest pub to the A592. Turn right onto the A592 to go to Patterdale.

# Day 8

# Patterdale to Patterdale

**17.9km (11.2 miles) distance - 845m (2789 feet) ascent - 950m (3135 feet) max altitude**

**Summary:** From Patterdale, walk north on the A592 to Grisedale Bridge and turn left up the road into Grisedale. At the end of the public road just before Thornhow, cross Grisedale Beck on the bridge and take the public footpath heading straight up towards Brownend Plantation. Follow the public footpath that head west up to the wall and cross the wall then bear west again, following the wall to the top of BIRKHOUSE MOOR which is just after the corner of the wall. Follow the path south-west to Hole-in-the-Wall where you head west over to Red Tarn. Climb diagonally west to the col between Swirral Edge and CATSTYE CAM. Turn north-east and climb the ridge to CATSYE CAM. Descend back to the col and climb Swirral Edge to HELVELLYN. From here, head south to NETHERMOST PIKE and continue over High Crag to DOLLYWAGGON PIKE. Then, a steep, zig-zag path takes you down to the eastern end of Grisedale Tarn and a long descent of Grisedale. Cross Grisedale Beck on the footbridge near the sheepfold to return to the tarmacked road at Thornhow. Now retrace your route from this morning back to your accommodation in Patterdale.

| MAPS | WAINWRIGHTS | M | FEET |
|---|---|---|---|
| OL5 | BIRKHOUSE MOOR | 718 | 2369 |
| | CATSTYE CAM | 890 | 2937 |
| | HELVELLYN | 950 | 3135 |
| | NETHERMOST PIKE | 891 | 2940 |
| | DOLLYWAGGON PIKE | 858 | 2831 |

## Patterdale to Hole-in-the-Wall (via BIRKHOUSE MOOR)

**5km (3.1 miles) distance - 570m (1881 feet) ascent**

**Route:** Walk north on the A592 to Grisedale Bridge and then go left up the lane that says there is no public parking on it. At the top of the lane it bears right across a bridge, follow it. Go through the gate ahead and steeply up to another gate, go through it. Turn left but then take the path that instantly rises diagonally ahead (not the path that stays quite level). Ignore the first path that cuts across you, but take the second opportunity to take a path off up to the right, this then soon kicks back left and you are now effectively just above the path you were on. (If you miss the right turn off to get you onto this higher path, you can follow the other path up to Hole-in-the-Wall and from there you could cross the wall that runs north-east/south-west and follow the path north-west to BIRKHOUSE MOOR and then return to Hole-in-the-Wall to continue the next section below.) The path is quite level and passes the corner of a fence. Then you rise diagonally to cross a fence at the stile. Follow the path diagonally up the hillside below some small crags until a faint path cuts across leading you right, to the wall. Cross the stone stile and just ahead of you, turn left to pick up the path climbing by the wall. (Part way up you can take a path that forks off to the right (not the one that goes down Mires Beck for Glenridding) if you want to visit a viewpoint near BIRKHOUSE MOOR, but that is not the summit.) At the top of the wall it turns south-west and, shortly afterwards, a cairn by the wall marks the true summit. Follow the wall to where the path forks, marked by a cairn, and there is a stile over the wall.

**ROUTE MAP: PATTERDALE TO PATTERDALE**

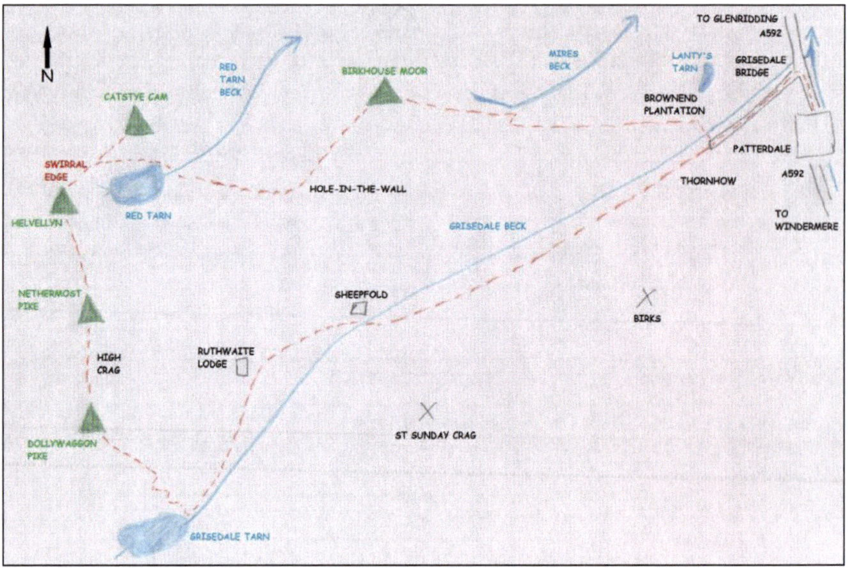


## Hole-in-the-Wall to CATSTYE CAM

**1.8km (1.1 miles) distance - 190m (625 feet) ascent**

**Route:** Bear right, downhill slightly. The path then levels out and rises gently to Red Tarn. Cross the outlet stream and you can go either left or right to get onto the path to Swirral Edge that runs diagonally up the flank of CATSTYE CAM ahead of you. Follow this path up to the ridge, but just before the ridge you can turn right to cut the corner and join the path up the ridge to the unmistakable peak of CATSTYE CAM which has a cairn.

Follow Standard 9-Day Itinerary, Day 8 from CATSTYE CAM to NETHERMOST PIKE (pg 55).

## NETHERMOST PIKE to DOLLYWAGGON PIKE

**1.5km (1 mile) distance - 60m (198 feet) ascent**

**Route:** Leave the summit cairn at about 200º and follow the edge onto High Crag which is marked by a large cairn. (If you prefer, High Crag can be bypassed on a path to the right of it.) Continue along the ridge (or path) to a col. Shortly after the col take the left-hand path at the fork to climb and follow the edge which begins to swing left over to DOLLYWAGGON PIKE. There is a very small dip in the route before the final climb. (If you take the right-hand path after the col, you will miss DOLLYWAGGON PIKE.) The summit is the cairn on the promontory to the north-east of the other cairn.

## DOLLYWAGGON PIKE to Patterdale

**7.6km (4.8 mile) distance - 20m (66 feet) ascent**

**Route:** Follow Standard 9-Day Itinerary, Day 4 from DOLLYWAGGON PIKE to ** (pg 43).

Pick up the path that leads all the way down Grisedale. After you pass Ruthwaite Lodge, ignore the first footbridge to your left and cross the 2nd one ahead. Continue along the path and eventually it becomes tarmac. (To avoid more ascent after a tough day, ignore the 3 footpaths to the right that you will see – the first of which is signposted for Patterdale. In order, these would add 50m, 40m and 30m of climbing. Also, if you have already changed into your trainers, then these paths are to be ignored.) The tarmac will now lead you down the way you came up this morning to the A592 main road and it is then right for Patterdale.

## Day 9

## Patterdale to Ambleside

Follow Standard 9-Day Itinerary, Day 9 (pg 56 - 59).

# STANDARD, NO BROTHERS WATER 8-DAY ITINERARY

## SUMMARY

**Day 1** is a circular combination of Days 1 and 2 from the Standard 9-Day Itinerary. You head out over RED SCREES, MIDDLE DODD, LITTLE HART CRAG and HIGH HARTSOP DODD then return over DOVE CRAG, HIGH PIKE and LOW PIKE to Ambleside. 7 Wainwrights done.

**Days 2 to 8** are the same as for the Standard 9-Day Itinerary, Days 3 to 9 (pg 30). 35 Wainwrights done!!!

## Day 1

## Ambleside to Ambleside

**18.9km (11.8 miles) distance - 1280m (4224 feet) ascent - 792m (2614 feet) max altitude**

**Summary:** From Ambleside, pick up the public footpath that joins Kirkstone Rd at the 150m contour. Leave the road at the 230m contour and climb the ridge over Snarker Pike to RED SCREES. Then descend to MIDDLE DODD. Now go back up Smallthwaite Band by the wall to take the path by the wall running north-west down to Scandale Pass. Follow up the other side and swing around onto the summit of LITTLE HART CRAG. From there, descend the ridge north-east to HIGH HARTSOP DODD. Now turn around again and go back up to bypass LITTLE HART CRAG to the north. Use the public footpath to cross Bakestones Moss and then climb to DOVE CRAG (with an optional detour to the viewpoint at High Bakestones). Then, heading south, descend the ridge over HIGH PIKE and LOW PIKE, past High Brock Crags and Low Brock Crags, past High Sweden Bridge and over Low Sweden Bridge, past Nook End Farm and back to Ambleside for an overnight stay.

| MAPS | WAINWRIGHTS | M | FEET |
|---|---|---|---|
| OL7 | RED SCREES | 776 | 2561 |
| | MIDDLE DODD | 654 | 2158 |
| | LITTLE HART CRAG | 637 | 2102 |
| | HIGH HARTSOP DODD | 519 | 1713 |
| | DOVE CRAG | 792 | 2614 |
| | HIGH PIKE | 656 | 2165 |
| | LOW PIKE | 508 | 1676 |

## ITINERARY MAP: STANDARD, NO BROTHERS WATER

## 8-DAY ITINERARY

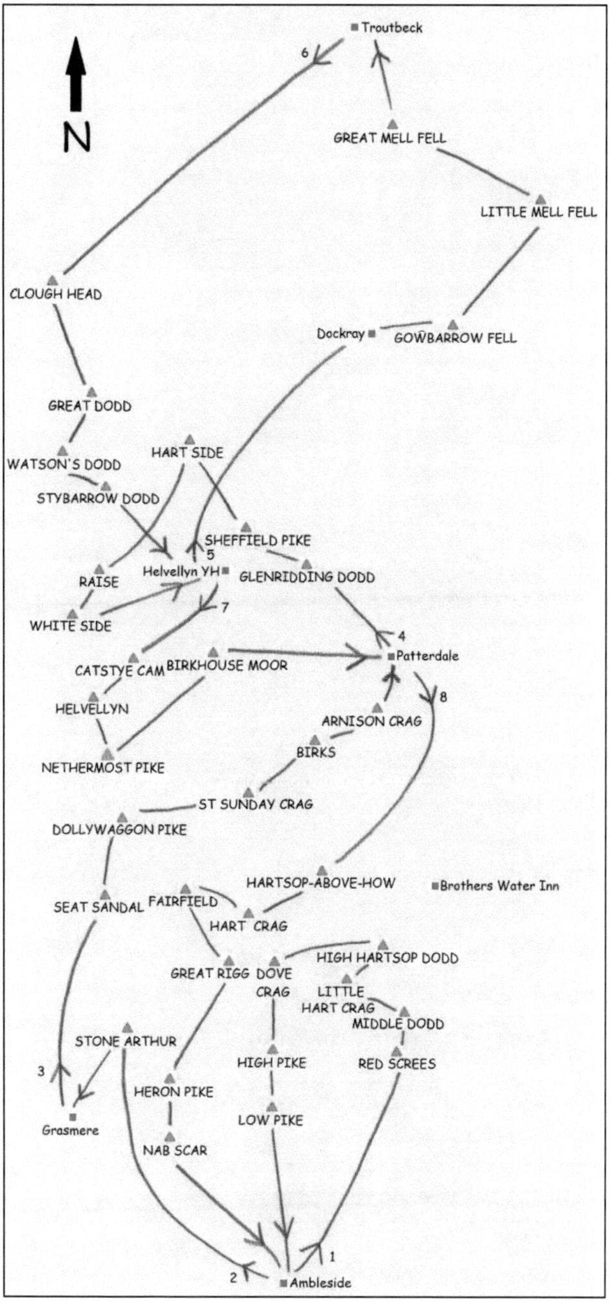

## DISTANCES, ASCENTS AND MAXIMUM ALTITUDES:

## STANDARD, NO BROTHERS WATER 8-DAY ITINERARY

| DAY | FROM | TO | DISTANCE | | ASCENT | | MAX ALTITUDE | |
|---|---|---|---|---|---|---|---|---|
| | | | KM | MILES | M | FEET | M | FEET |
| 1 | AMBLESIDE | AMBLESIDE | 18.9 | 11.8 | 1280 | 4224 | 792 | 2614 |
| 2 | AMBLESIDE | GRASMERE | 9.9 | 6.2 | 500 | 1650 | 500 | 1650 |
| 3 | GRASMERE | PATTERDALE | 14.3 | 8.9 | 1355 | 4472 | 858 | 2831 |
| 4 | PATTERDALE | HELVELLYN YH | 14.7 | 9.2 | 980 | 3234 | 883 | 2914 |
| 5 | HELVELLYN YH | TROUTBECK | 20.3 | 12.7 | 1130 | 3729 | 630 | 2079 |
| 6 | TROUTBECK | HELVELLYN YH | 20.6 | 12.9 | 870 | 2871 | 857 | 2828 |
| 7 | HELVELLYN YH | PATTERDALE | 11.5 | 7.2 | 870 | 2871 | 950 | 3135 |
| 8 | PATTERDALE | AMBLESIDE | 15.5 | 9.7 | 845 | 2789 | 873 | 2881 |
| | | **TOTALS** | **125.7** | **78.6** | **7830** | **25839** | | |

## ROUTE MAP: AMBLESIDE TO AMBLESIDE

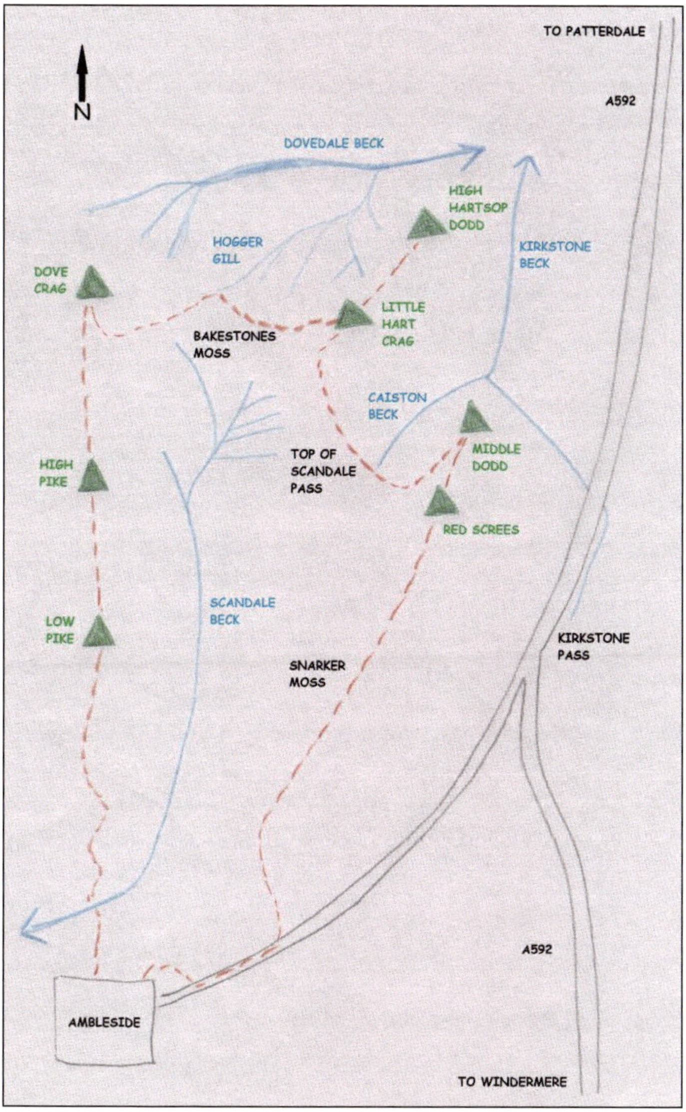


# Ambleside to MIDDLE DODD

**6.7km (4.2 miles) distance - 735m (2426 feet) ascent**

Follow Standard 9-Day Itinerary, Day 1 to MIDDLE DODD (pg 33 - 34).

## MIDDLE DODD to LITTLE HART CRAG

**2.5km (1.6 miles) distance - 200m (660 feet) ascent**

**Route:** Turn round and return to the corner of the wall. Follow the wall back south-west until another wall comes off to the right downhill at about 305°. Follow this wall down to the col at Scandale Pass. From the col follow the wall up to its corner and then just above Scandale Tarn to your left, bear right and approach LITTLE HART CRAG summit from the back by going round the left of it.

## LITTLE HART CRAG to HIGH HARTSOP DODD

**1km (0.6 miles) distance - 0m (0 feet) ascent**

**Route:** Go down the ridge roughly north-north-east and the 'summit' is marked by a small cairn just before the ground drops a little more steeply to the wall.

## HIGH HARTSOP DODD to Ambleside

**8.7km (5.4 miles) distance - 345m (1139 feet) ascent**

**Route:** Follow Standard 9-Day Itinerary, Day 2 from HIGH HARTSOP DODD to Ambleside but miss out the summit of LITTLE HART CRAG (pg 37 - 38).

## Days 2 to 8

## Ambleside to Ambleside

Follow Standard 9-Day Itinerary, Days 3 to 9 (pg 38 - 59).

# DOCKRAY, NO BROTHERS WATER 8-DAY ITINERARY

## SUMMARY

**Day 1** is the same as for the Standard, No Brothers Water 8-Day Itinerary (pg 78). 7 Wainwrights done.

**Days 2 to 8** are the same as for the Dockray 9-Day Itinerary, Days 3 to 9 (pg 60). 35 Wainwrights done!!!

### Day 1

### Ambleside to Ambleside

Follow Standard, No Brothers Water 8-Day Itinerary, Day 1 (pg 78 - 82).

### Days 2 to 8

### Ambleside to Ambleside

Follow Dockray 9-Day Itinerary, Days 3 to 9 (pg 60 - 68).

*St Sunday Crag from Seat Sandal*

## ITINERARY MAP: DOCKRAY, NO BROTHERS WATER

### 8-DAY ITINERARY

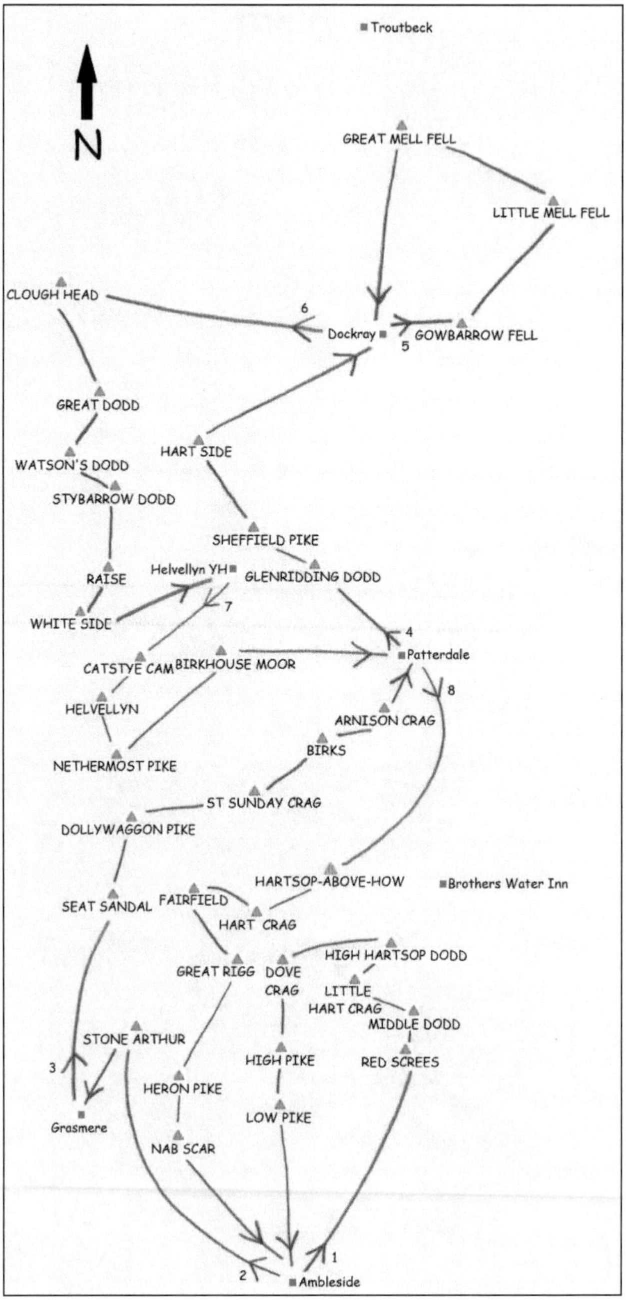

## DISTANCES, ASCENTS AND MAXIMUM ALTITUDES:

## DOCKRAY, NO BROTHERS WATER 8-DAY ITINERARY

| DAY | FROM | TO | DISTANCE KM | DISTANCE MILES | ASCENT M | ASCENT FEET | MAX ALTITUDE M | MAX ALTITUDE FEET |
|---|---|---|---|---|---|---|---|---|
| 1 | AMBLESIDE | AMBLESIDE | 18.9 | 11.8 | 1280 | 4224 | 792 | 2614 |
| 2 | AMBLESIDE | GRASMERE | 9.9 | 6.2 | 500 | 1650 | 500 | 1650 |
| 3 | GRASMERE | PATTERDALE | 14.3 | 8.9 | 1355 | 4472 | 858 | 2831 |
| 4 | PATTERDALE | DOCKRAY | 12 | 7.5 | 770 | 2541 | 756 | 2495 |
| 5 | DOCKRAY | DOCKRAY | 17.6 | 11 | 830 | 2739 | 537 | 1772 |
| 6 | DOCKRAY | HELVELLYN YH | 17 | 10.6 | 1020 | 3366 | 883 | 2914 |
| 7 | HELVELLYN YH | PATTERDALE | 11.5 | 7.2 | 870 | 2871 | 950 | 3135 |
| 8 | PATTERDALE | AMBLESIDE | 15.5 | 9.7 | 845 | 2789 | 873 | 2881 |
| | | **TOTALS** | **116.7** | **72.9** | **7470** | **24651** | | |

# EDGES, NO BROTHERS WATER 8-DAY ITINERARY

## SUMMARY

**Day 1** is the same as for the Standard, No Brothers Water 8-Day Itinerary (pg 78). 7 Wainwrights done.

**Days 2 to 8** are the same as for the Edges 9-Day Itinerary, Days 3 to 9 (pg 69 - 77). 35 Wainwrights done!!!

## Day 1

## Ambleside to Ambleside

Follow Standard, No Brothers Water 8-Day Itinerary, Day 1 (pg 78 - 82).

*High Pike from Red Screes*

## Days 2 to 8

## Ambleside to Ambleside

Follow Edges 9-Day Itinerary, Days 3 to 9 (pg 69 - 77).

## ITINERARY MAP: EDGES, NO BROTHERS WATER

## 8-DAY ITINERARY

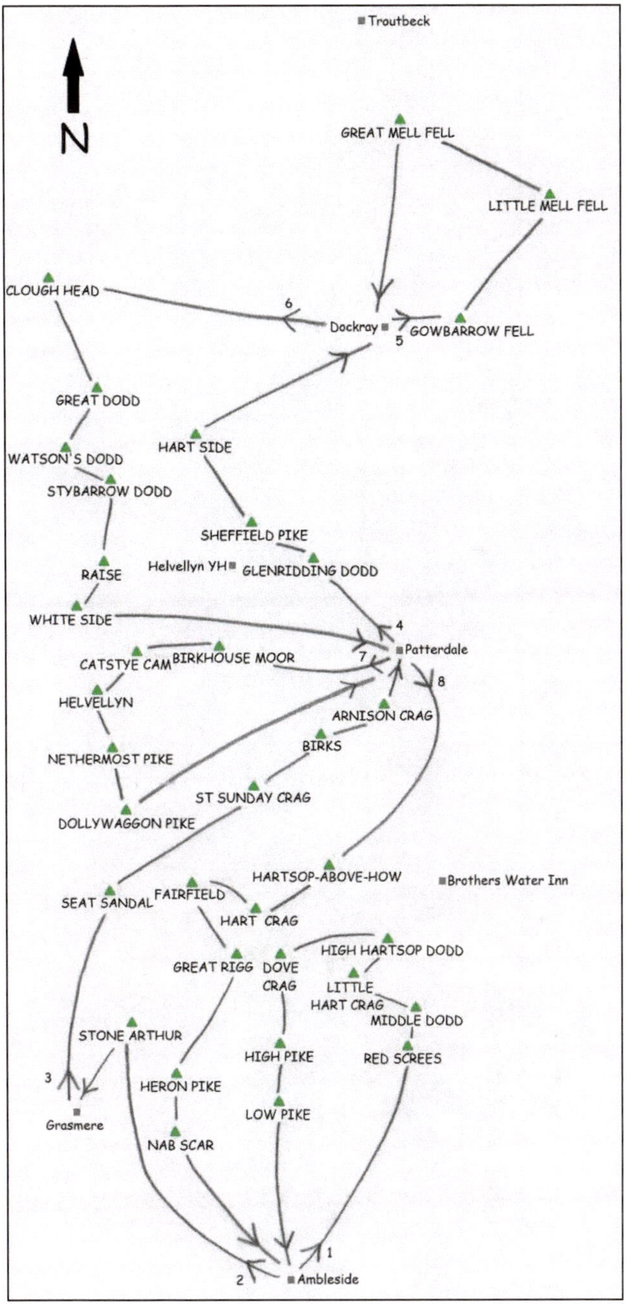

## DISTANCES, ASCENTS AND MAXIMUM ALTITUDES:

## EDGES, NO BROTHERS WATER 8-DAY ITINERARY

| DAY | FROM | TO | DISTANCE | | ASCENT | | MAX ALTITUDE | |
|---|---|---|---|---|---|---|---|---|
| | | | KM | MILES | M | FEET | M | FEET |
| 1 | AMBLESIDE | AMBLESIDE | 18.9 | 11.8 | 1280 | 4224 | 792 | 2614 |
| 2 | AMBLESIDE | GRASMERE | 9.9 | 6.2 | 500 | 1650 | 500 | 1650 |
| 3 | GRASMERE | PATTERDALE | 14.3 | 8.9 | 1355 | 4472 | 858 | 2831 |
| 4 | PATTERDALE | DOCKRAY | 12 | 7.5 | 770 | 2541 | 756 | 2495 |
| 5 | DOCKRAY | DOCKRAY | 17.6 | 11 | 830 | 2739 | 537 | 1772 |
| 6 | DOCKRAY | HELVELLYN YH | 17 | 10.6 | 1020 | 3366 | 883 | 2914 |
| 7 | HELVELLYN YH | PATTERDALE | 11.5 | 7.2 | 870 | 2871 | 950 | 3135 |
| 8 | PATTERDALE | AMBLESIDE | 15.5 | 9.7 | 845 | 2789 | 873 | 2881 |
| | | **TOTALS** | **116.7** | **72.9** | **7470** | **24651** | | |

# STANDARD, NO AMBLESIDE 8-DAY ITINERARY

## SUMMARY

**Day 1** is the same as for the Standard 9-Day Itinerary (pg 30). 2 Wainwrights done.

**Day 2** is a combination of Days 2 and 3 from the Standard 9-Day Itinerary. You leave Brothers water and travel over HIGH HARTSOP DODD, LITTLE HART CRAG, DOVE CRAG, HIGH PIKE, LOW PIKE and finally take in STONE ARTHUR before arriving in Grasmere for the night. 8 Wainwrights done.

**Days 3 to 8** are the same as for the Standard 9-Day Itinerary, days 4 to 9 (pg 30). 35 Wainwrights done!!!

## Day 1

### Ambleside to Brothers Water Inn

Follow Standard 9-Day Itinerary, Day 1 (pg 33 - 35).

## Day 2

### Brothers Water Inn to Grasmere

**16.5km (10.3 miles) distance - 1185m (3911 feet) ascent - 792m (2614 feet) max altitude**

**Summary:** From the Brothers Water Inn, head back past Hartsop Hall and take the public footpath south to the foot of the ridge up to HIGH HARTSOP DODD. Climb it and continue up to LITTLE HART CRAG. Use the public footpath to cross Bakestones Moss and then climb to DOVE CRAG (with an optional detour to the viewpoint at High Bakestones). Then, heading south, descend the ridge over HIGH PIKE and LOW PIKE, past High Brock Crags and Low Brock Crags, past High Sweden Bridge and just before Low Sweden Bridge, turn west to drop down onto the path through Rydal Park and past Rydal Hall. This brings you to the low-level Coffin Route which you take below NAB SCAR (not ticked off until Day 9), past Town End to the outskirts of Grasmere near Michael's Fold. From there, a steep climb on the public footpath takes you up to STONE ARTHUR. Descending the same way takes you back to Grasmere for the night.

## ITINERARY MAP: STANDARD, NO AMBLESIDE 8-DAY ITINERARY

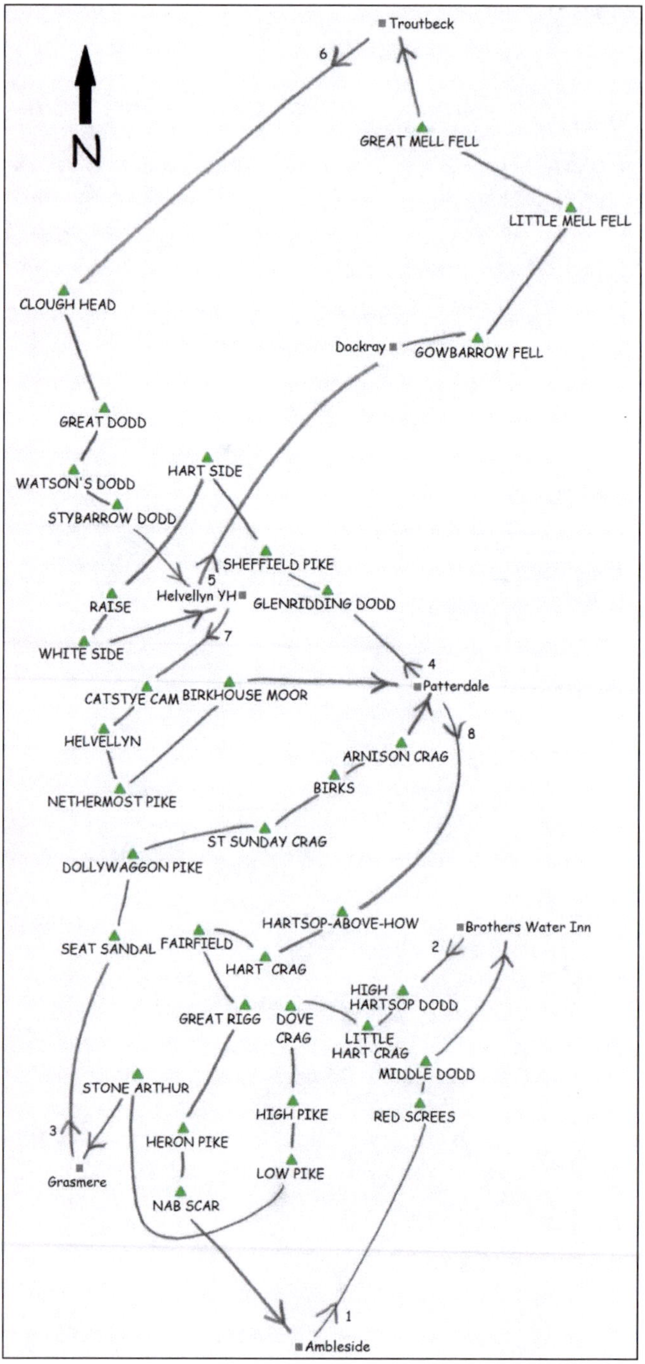

## DISTANCES, ASCENTS AND MAXIMUM ALTITUDES:

## STANDARD, NO AMBLESIDE 8-DAY ITINERARY

| DAY | FROM | TO | DISTANCE | | ASCENT | | MAX ALTITUDE | |
|---|---|---|---|---|---|---|---|---|
| | | | KM | MILES | M | FEET | M | FEET |
| 1 | AMBLESIDE | BROTHERS WATER INN | 9.8 | 6.1 | 745 | 2459 | 776 | 2561 |
| 2 | BROTHERS WATER INN | GRASMERE | 16.5 | 10.3 | 1185 | 3911 | 792 | 2614 |
| 3 | GRASMERE | PATTERDALE | 14.3 | 8.9 | 1355 | 4472 | 858 | 2831 |
| 4 | PATTERDALE | HELVELLYN YH | 14.7 | 9.2 | 980 | 3234 | 883 | 2914 |
| 5 | HELVELLYN YH | TROUTBECK | 20.3 | 12.7 | 1130 | 3729 | 630 | 2079 |
| 6 | TROUTBECK | HELVELLYN YH | 20.6 | 12.9 | 870 | 2871 | 857 | 2828 |
| 7 | HELVELLYN YH | PATTERDALE | 11.5 | 7.2 | 870 | 2871 | 950 | 3135 |
| 8 | PATTERDALE | AMBLESIDE | 15.5 | 9.7 | 845 | 2789 | 873 | 2881 |
| | | **TOTALS** | **123.2** | **77** | **7980** | **26334** | | |

## ROUTE MAP: BROTHERS WATER INN TO GRASMERE

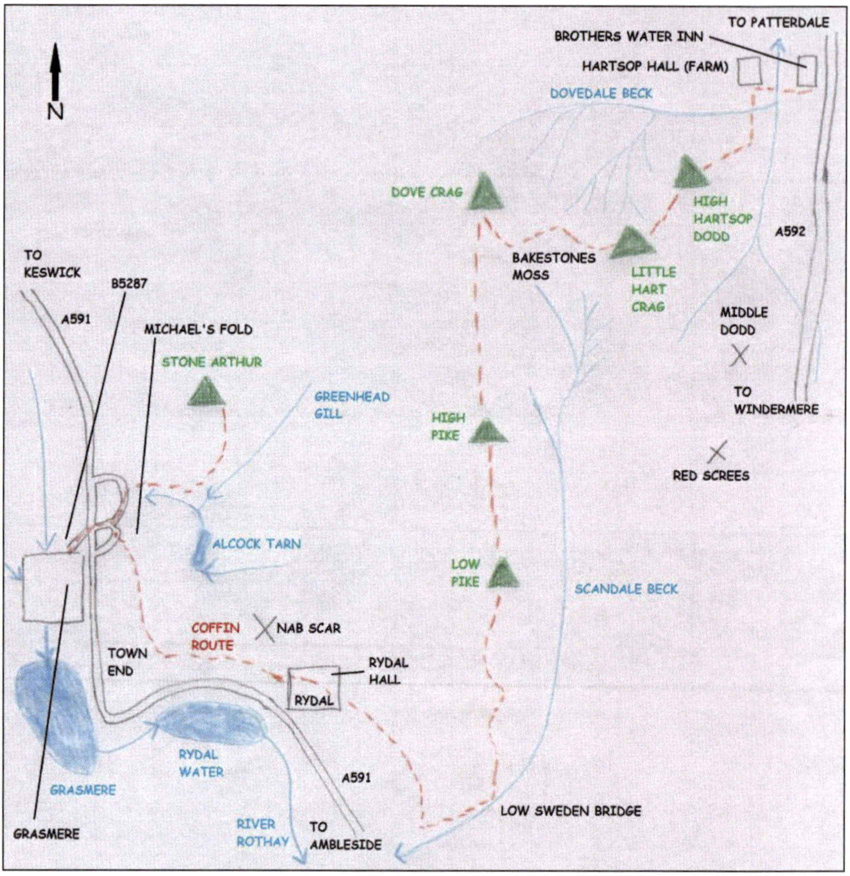


| MAPS | WAINWRIGHTS | M | FEET |
|---|---|---|---|
| OL5, OL7 | HIGH HARTSOP DODD | 519 | 1713 |
| | LITTLE HART CRAG | 637 | 2102 |
| | DOVE CRAG | 792 | 2614 |
| | HIGH PIKE | 656 | 2165 |
| | LOW PIKE | 508 | 1676 |
| | STONE ARTHUR | 500 | 1650 |

## Brothers Water Inn to Low Sweden Bridge

**9.7km (6.1 miles) distance - 695m (2294 feet) ascent**

Follow Standard 9-Day Itinerary, Day 2 to * (pg 35 - 38).

## Low Sweden Bridge to Rydal Hall Path

**0.3km (0.2 miles) distance - 0m (0 feet) ascent**

**Route:** Follow the wall to the right down to the gate in the corner of the field. Go through the gate. Descend through the trees to meet the Ambleside-Rydal Hall path. Turn right.

## Rydal Hall Path to Grasmere

**6.5km (4.1 miles) distance - 490m (1617 feet) ascent**

Follow Standard 9-Day Itinerary, Day 3 from * (pg 39 - 40).

## Days 3 to 8

## Grasmere to Ambleside

Follow Standard 9-Day Itinerary, Days 4 to 9 (pg 41 - 59).

*Seat Sandal from Thorney How*

# DOCKRAY, NO AMBLESIDE 8-DAY ITINERARY

## SUMMARY

**Day 1** is the same as for the Standard 9-Day Itinerary (pg 30). 2 Wainwrights done.

**Day 2** is the same as for the Standard, No Ambleside 8-Day Itinerary (pg 89). 8 Wainwrights done.

**Days 3 to 8** are the same as for the Dockray 9-Day Itinerary, Days 4 to 9 (pg 60). 35 Wainwrights done!!!

## Day 1

### Ambleside to Brothers Water Inn

Follow Standard 9-Day Itinerary, Day 1 (pg 33 - 35).

## Day 2

### Brothers Water Inn to Grasmere

Follow Standard, No Ambleside 8-Day Itinerary, Day 2 (pg 89 - 93).

## Days 3 to 8

### Grasmere to Ambleside

Follow Dockray 9-Day Itinerary, Days 4 to 9 (pg 60 - 68).

## ITINERARY MAP: DOCKRAY, NO AMBLESIDE 8-DAY ITINERARY

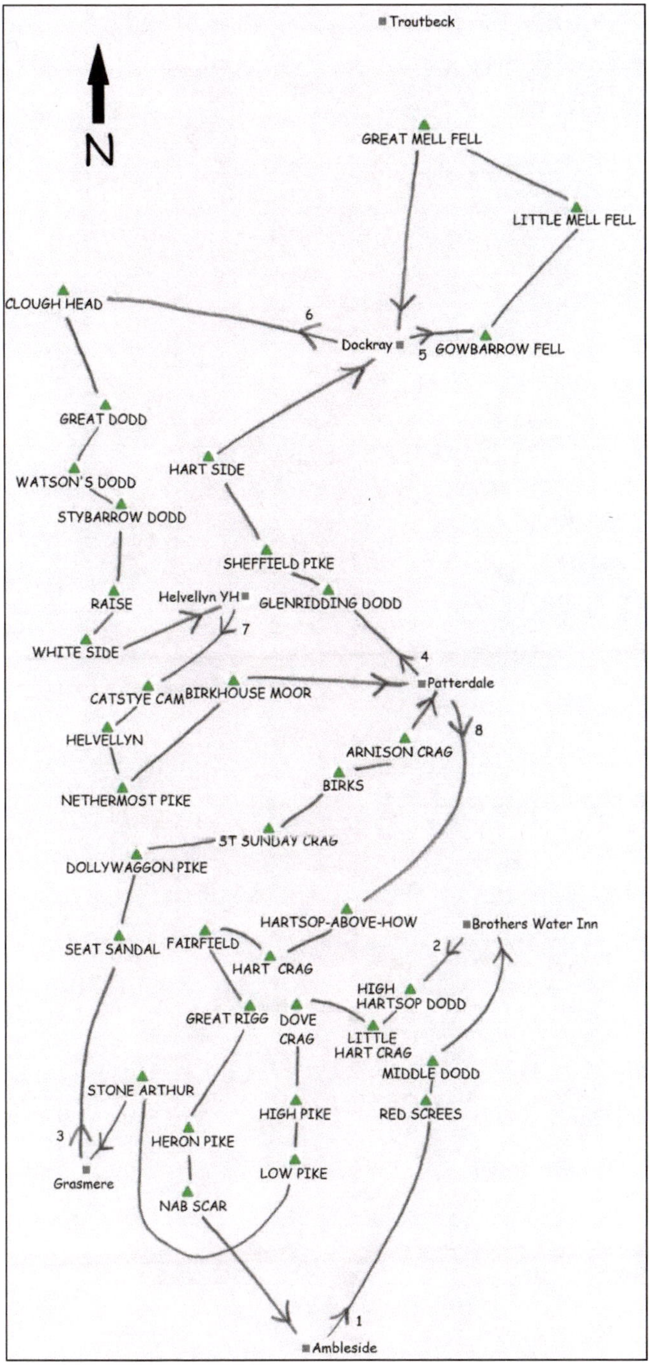

## DISTANCES, ASCENTS AND MAXIMUM ALTITUDES:

## DOCKRAY, NO AMBLESIDE 8-DAY ITINERARY

| DAY | FROM | TO | DISTANCE KM | DISTANCE MILES | ASCENT M | ASCENT FEET | MAX ALTITUDE M | MAX ALTITUDE FEET |
|---|---|---|---|---|---|---|---|---|
| 1 | AMBLESIDE | BROTHERS WATER INN | 9.8 | 6.1 | 745 | 2459 | 776 | 2561 |
| 2 | BROTHERS WATER INN | GRASMERE | 16.5 | 10.3 | 1185 | 3911 | 792 | 2614 |
| 3 | GRASMERE | PATTERDALE | 14.3 | 8.9 | 1355 | 4472 | 858 | 2831 |
| 4 | PATTERDALE | DOCKRAY | 12 | 7.5 | 770 | 2541 | 756 | 2495 |
| 5 | DOCKRAY | DOCKRAY | 17.6 | 11 | 830 | 2739 | 537 | 1772 |
| 6 | DOCKRAY | HELVELLYN YH | 17 | 10.6 | 1020 | 3366 | 883 | 2914 |
| 7 | HELVELLYN YH | PATTERDALE | 11.5 | 7.2 | 870 | 2871 | 950 | 3135 |
| 8 | PATTERDALE | AMBLESIDE | 15.5 | 9.7 | 845 | 2789 | 873 | 2881 |
| | | TOTALS | 114.2 | 71.4 | 7620 | 25146 | | |

# EDGES, NO AMBLESIDE 8-DAY ITINERARY

## SUMMARY

**Day 1** is the same as for the Standard 9-Day Itinerary (pg 30). 2 Wainwrights done.

**Day 2** is the same as for the Standard, No Ambleside 8-Day Itinerary (pg 89). 8 Wainwrights done.

**Days 3 to 8** are the same as for the Edges 9-Day Itinerary, Days 4 to 9 (pg 69). 35 Wainwrights done!!!

## Day 1

### Ambleside to Brothers Water Inn

Follow Standard 9-Day Itinerary, Day 1 (pg 33 - 35).

## Day 2

### Brothers Water Inn to Grasmere

Follow Standard, No Ambleside 8-Day Itinerary, Day 2 (pg 89 - 93).

## Days 3 to 8

### Grasmere to Ambleside

Follow Edges 9-Day Itinerary, Days 4 to 9 (pg 69 - 77).

## ITINERARY MAP: EDGES, NO AMBLESIDE 8-DAY ITINERARY

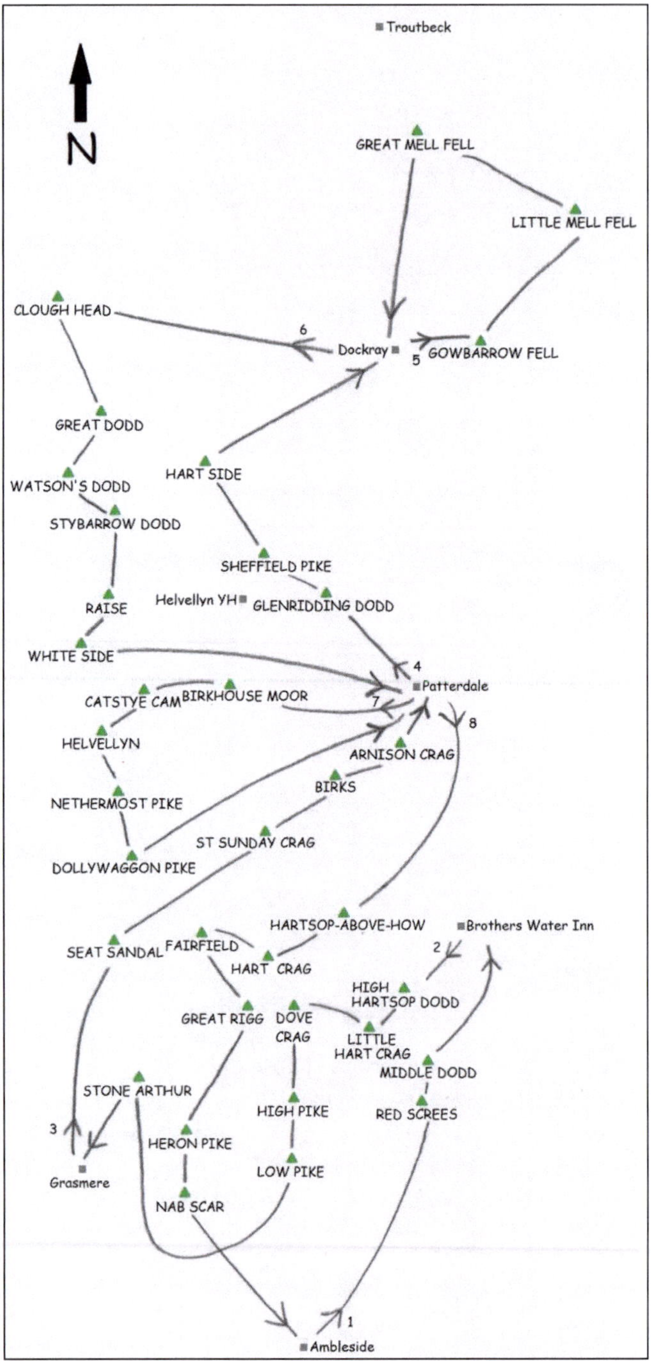

## DISTANCES, ASCENTS AND MAXIMUM ALTITUDES:

## EDGES, NO AMBLESIDE 8-DAY ITINERARY

| DAY | FROM | TO | DISTANCE | | ASCENT | | MAX ALTITUDE | |
|---|---|---|---|---|---|---|---|---|
| | | | KM | MILES | M | FEET | M | FEET |
| 1 | AMBLESIDE | BROTHERS WATER INN | 9.8 | 6.1 | 745 | 2459 | 776 | 2561 |
| 2 | BROTHERS WATER INN | GRASMERE | 16.5 | 10.3 | 1185 | 3911 | 792 | 2614 |
| 3 | GRASMERE | PATTERDALE | 12.6 | 7.9 | 1075 | 3548 | 841 | 2775 |
| 4 | PATTERDALE | DOCKRAY | 12 | 7.5 | 770 | 2541 | 756 | 2495 |
| 5 | DOCKRAY | DOCKRAY | 17.6 | 11 | 830 | 2739 | 537 | 1772 |
| 6 | DOCKRAY | PATTERDALE | 21.1 | 13.2 | 1020 | 3366 | 883 | 2914 |
| 7 | PATTERDALE | PATTERDALE | 17.9 | 11.2 | 1000 | 3300 | 950 | 3135 |
| 8 | PATTERDALE | AMBLESIDE | 15.5 | 9.7 | 845 | 2789 | 873 | 2881 |
| | | **TOTALS** | **123** | **76.9** | **7470** | **24651** | | |

# NO BROTHERS WATER 7-DAY ITINERARY

## SUMMARY

**Days 1 to 3** are the same as for the Dockray, No Brothers Water 8-Day Itinerary (pg 83). 8 Wainwrights done.

**Day 4** is a combination of Dockray 9-Day Itinerary, Day 5 and the second half of Standard 9-Day Itinerary, Day 6. It takes you over GLENRIDDING DODD, SHEFFIELD PIKE and HART SIDE before dropping you into the hamlet of Dockray from where you head over GOWBARROW FELL, LITTLE MELL FELL and GREAT MELL FELL to an overnight stay at the tiny hamlet of Troutbeck. 14 Wainwrights done.

**Day 5** begins the same as Standard 9-Day Itinerary, Day 7 then becomes the same as Dockray 9-Day Itinerary, Day 7. It covers CLOUGH HEAD, GREAT DODD, WATSON'S DODD, STYBARROW DODD, RAISE and WHITE SIDE before dropping to Helvellyn YH for the night. 20 Wainwrights done.

**Days 6 to 7** are the same as for the Standard 9-Day Itinerary, Days 8 to 9 (pg 30). 35 Wainwrights done!!!

## Days 1 to 3

## Ambleside to Patterdale

Follow Dockray, No Brothers Water 8-Day Itinerary, Days 1 to 3 (pg 83).

## Day 4

## Patterdale to Troutbeck

**25.2km (15.8 miles) distance - 1530m (5049 feet) ascent - 756m (2495 feet) max altitude**

**Summary:** From Patterdale, a short stretch of road-walking north on the A592 takes you to Glenridding and just after Glenridding Bridge you turn left up the road past the Travellers Rest pub to the foot of Blaes Crag. You ascend The Rake north to the wall and then a short return journey to the east ticks off GLENRIDDING DODD. From The Rake, you now head north-west over Heron pike to SHEFFIELD PIKE. You now drop to Nick Head and then climb to the east of the disused quarries to head north above Glencoyne Head. This leads you across the col to the summit of HART SIDE. Head over the col and rising ground to the south-east and follow the wall down to pick up the public footpath that passes Brown Hills, Swineside Knott and Common Fell all the way to Dockray. Cross the bridge on the A5091 and take the public footpath east down to cross Riddings Beck. Bear right and then follow up the southern side of the trees in the access land (there is a clear path) to the summit of GOWBARROW FELL. Continue round to the shooting lodge and take the public footpath through the trees at Swinburn's Park and over to the road near Underwood. A short stretch of road-walking takes you up to The Hause and a short, steep ascent takes you up LITTLE MELL FELL. Come back down to the road again and follow it, west then north, round to the little left-hand lane just after Brownrigg Farm. Follow the lane for a short way and then enter the access land and make the steady ascent up the broad ridge to the summit of GREAT MELL FELL. Carry on over and very steeply down to the disused rifle range which leads down to the A5091 and Troutbeck.

Refer to 'ROUTE MAP: PATTERDALE TO DOCKRAY' of Dockray 9-Day Itinerary, Day 5 (pg 63).

Refer to 'ROUTE MAP B: DOCKRAY TO TROUTBECK' of Standard 9-Day Itinerary, Day 6 (pg 49).

| MAPS | WAINWRIGHTS | M | FEET |
|---|---|---|---|
| OL5 | GLENRIDDING DODD | 442 | 1459 |
| | SHEFFIELD PIKE | 675 | 2228 |
| | HART SIDE | 756 | 2495 |
| | GOWBARROW FELL | 481 | 1587 |
| | LITTLE MELL FELL | 505 | 1667 |
| | GREAT MELL FELL | 537 | 1772 |

Follow Dockray 9-Day Itinerary, Day 5 (pg 63 - 64).

## Dockray to Troutbeck

**13.2km (8.3 miles) distance - 760m (2508 feet) ascent**

Follow Standard 9-Day Itinerary, Day 6 from ** (pg 48 - 50).

## ITINERARY MAP: NO BROTHERS WATER 7-DAY ITINERARY

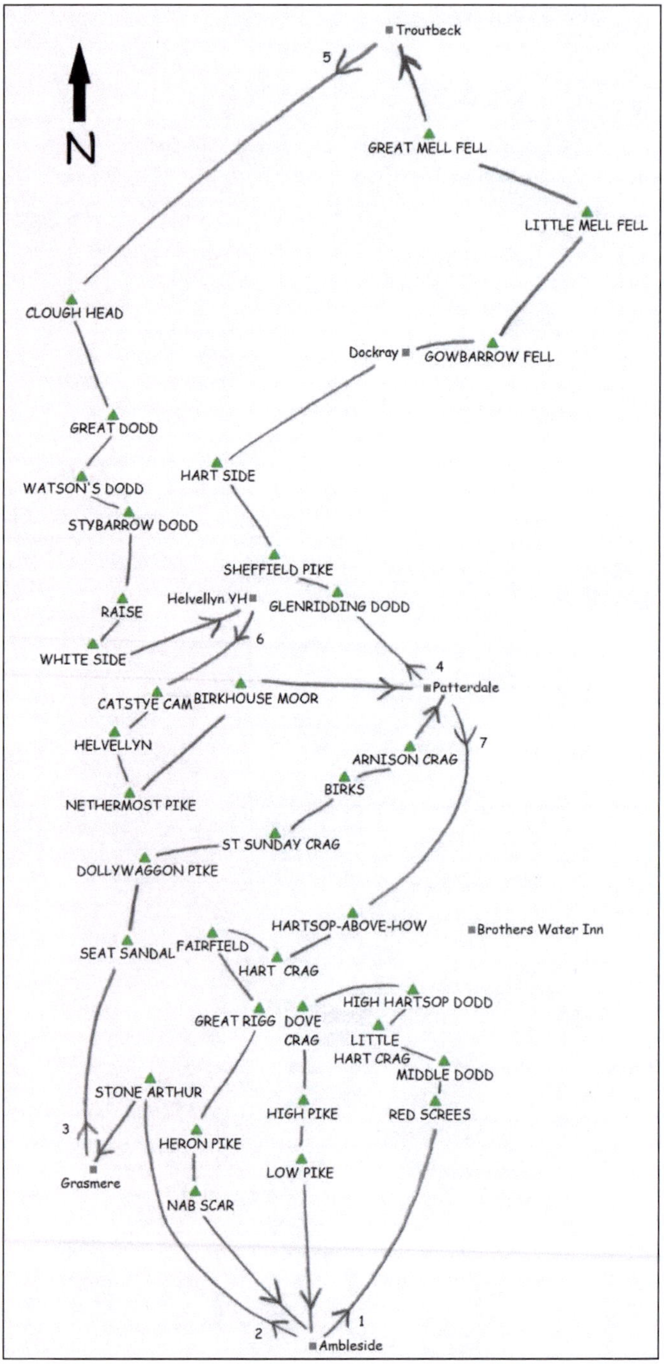

## DISTANCES, ASCENTS AND MAXIMUM ALTITUDES:

## NO BROTHERS WATER 7-DAY ITINERARY

| DAY | FROM | TO | DISTANCE | | ASCENT | | MAX ALTITUDE | |
|---|---|---|---|---|---|---|---|---|
| | | | KM | MILES | M | FEET | M | FEET |
| 1 | AMBLESIDE | AMBLESIDE | 18.9 | 11.8 | 1280 | 4224 | 792 | 2614 |
| 2 | AMBLESIDE | GRASMERE | 9.9 | 6.2 | 500 | 1650 | 500 | 1650 |
| 3 | GRASMERE | PATTERDALE | 14.3 | 8.9 | 1355 | 4472 | 858 | 2831 |
| 4 | PATTERDALE | TROUTBECK | 25.2 | 15.8 | 1530 | 5049 | 756 | 2495 |
| 5 | TROUTBECK | HELVELLYN YH | 21.5 | 13.4 | 1070 | 3531 | 883 | 2914 |
| 6 | HELVELLYN YH | PATTERDALE | 11.5 | 7.2 | 870 | 2871 | 950 | 3135 |
| 7 | PATTERDALE | AMBLESIDE | 15.5 | 9.7 | 845 | 2789 | 873 | 2881 |
| | | **TOTALS** | **116.8** | **73** | **7450** | **24585** | | |

# Day 5

## Troutbeck to Helvellyn YH

**21.5km (13.4miles) distance - 1070m (3531feet) ascent - 883m (2914feet) max altitude**

**Summary:** From Troutbeck, a stretch of road-walking on the A5091 takes you to Binks Moss and you turn right onto "New Road", which you take past Cockley Moor to the junction at Red Moss. Turn right onto the Old Coach Road which you follow between Wolfcrag Moss and Barbaryrigg Moss and over Mariel Bridge. Head up the ridge of White Pike but pass to the south of the crags to reach the north-east ridge of CLOUGH HEAD which you follow to the summit. You then head down towards Calfhow Pike, but cut the corner to swing up the ridge to GREAT DODD. A pleasant ridge walk takes you onto WATSON'S DODD. An easy climb takes you onto STYBARROW DODD, from where, head down to the top of Sticks Pass. Make the steady climb south to RAISE. From there, descend and climb south-west to WHITE SIDE (marked as Whiteside Bank) before turning back briefly and turning down to zig-zag down into Glenridding valley and follow down to Helvellyn YH.

Refer to 'ROUTE MAP A: TROUTBECK TO GREAT DODD' of Standard 9-Day Itinerary, Day 7 (pg 51).

**ROUTE MAP B: GREAT DODD TO WATSON'S DODD**

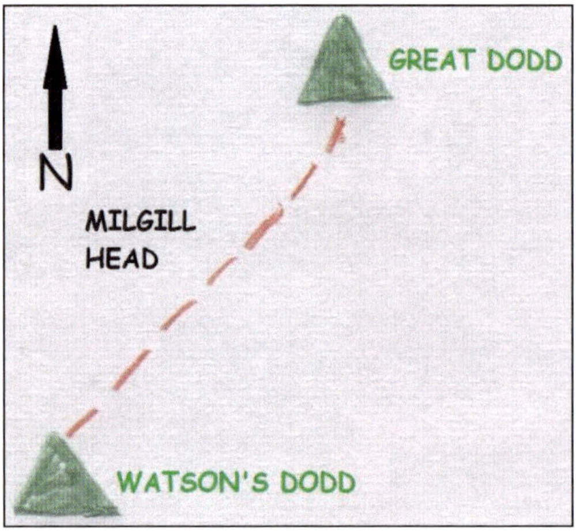


Refer to 'ROUTE MAP B: WATSON'S DODD TO HELVELLYN YH' of Dockray 9-Day Itinerary, Day 7 (pg 67).

| MAPS | WAINWRIGHTS | M | FEET |
|---|---|---|---|
| OL5 | CLOUGH HEAD | 726 | 2396 |
| | GREAT DODD | 857 | 2828 |
| | WATSON'S DODD | 789 | 2604 |
| | STYBARROW DODD | 843 | 2782 |
| | RAISE | 883 | 2914 |
| | WHITE SIDE | 863 | 2848 |

## Troutbeck to 'Old Coach Road'

**5.9km (3.7 miles) distance - 170m (561 feet) ascent**

Follow Standard 9-Day Itinerary, Day 7 to * (pg 50 - 51).

## 'Old Coach Road' to Helvellyn YH

**15.6km (9.7 miles) distance - 900m (2970 feet) ascent**

Follow Dockray 9-Day Itinerary, Day 7 from 'Old Coach Road' (pg 68).

## Days 6 to 7

## Helvellyn YH to Ambleside

Follow Standard 9-Day Itinerary, Days 8 to 9 (pg 53 - 59).

# NO AMBLESIDE 7-DAY ITINERARY

## SUMMARY

**Days 1 to 3** are the same as for the Dockray, No Ambleside 8-Day Itinerary (pg 94). 13 Wainwrights done.

**Days 4 to 7** are the same as for the No Brothers Water 7-Day Itinerary (pg 100). 35 Wainwrights done!!!

### Days 1 to 3

### Ambleside to Patterdale

Follow Dockray, No Ambleside 8-Day Itinerary, Days 1 to 3 (pg 94).

### Days 4 to 7

### Patterdale to Ambleside

Follow No Brothers Water 7-Day Itinerary, Days 4 to 7 (pg 100-105).

*Helvellyn from Red Tarn*

## ITINERARY MAP: NO AMBLESIDE 7-DAY ITINERARY

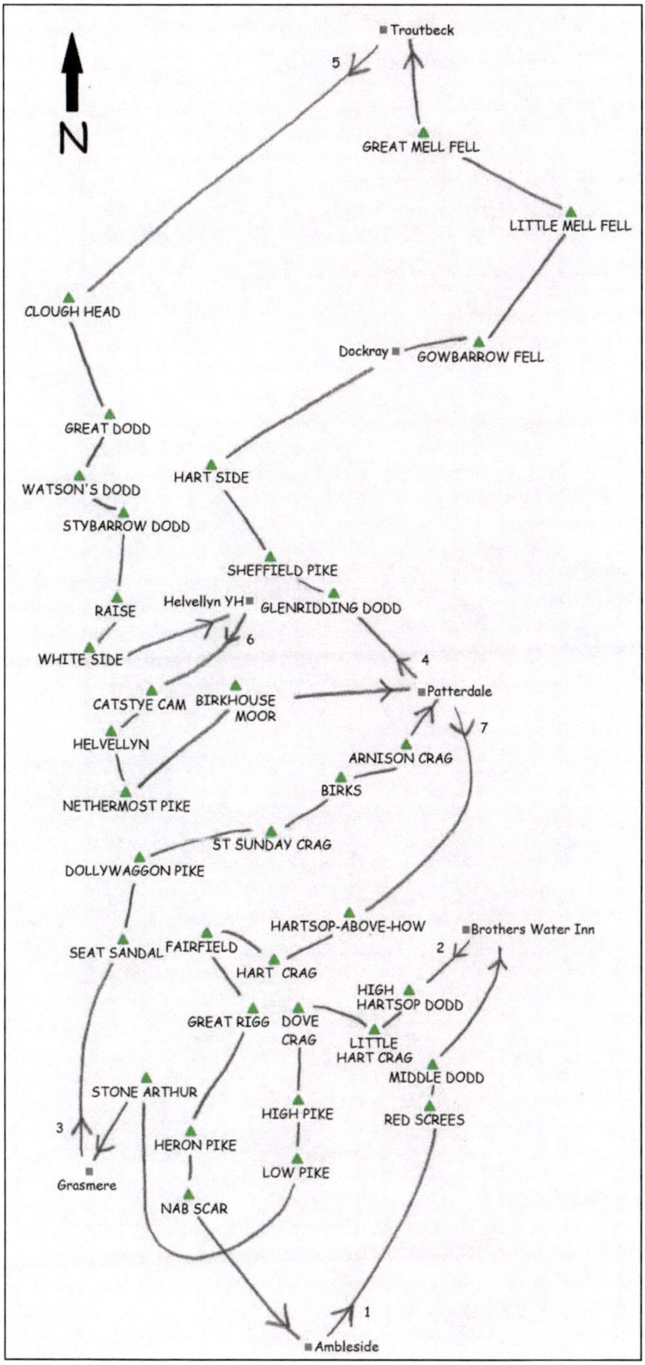

## DISTANCES, ASCENTS AND MAXIMUM ALTITUDES:

### NO AMBLESIDE 7-DAY ITINERARY

| DAY | FROM | TO | DISTANCE | | ASCENT | | MAX ALTITUDE | |
|---|---|---|---|---|---|---|---|---|
| | | | KM | MILES | M | FEET | M | FEET |
| 1 | AMBLESIDE | BROTHERS WATER INN | 9.8 | 6.1 | 745 | 2459 | 776 | 2561 |
| 2 | BROTHERS WATER INN | GRASMERE | 16.5 | 10.3 | 1185 | 3911 | 792 | 2614 |
| 3 | GRASMERE | PATTERDALE | 14.3 | 8.9 | 1355 | 4472 | 858 | 2831 |
| 4 | PATTERDALE | TROUTBECK | 25.2 | 15.8 | 1530 | 5049 | 756 | 2495 |
| 5 | TROUTBECK | HELVELLYN YH | 21.5 | 13.4 | 1070 | 3531 | 883 | 2914 |
| 6 | HELVELLYN YH | PATTERDALE | 11.5 | 7.2 | 870 | 2871 | 950 | 3135 |
| 7 | PATTERDALE | AMBLESIDE | 15.5 | 9.7 | 845 | 2789 | 873 | 2881 |
| | | **TOTALS** | **114.3** | **71.4** | **7600** | **25080** | | |

23599400R20060

Made in the USA
Charleston, SC
29 October 2013